# TRAILS OF MEMORY

## A Century of Nazism

## By Gaither Stewart

Cyberwit.net

HIG 45 Kaushambi Kunj, Kalindipuram

Allahabad - 211011 (U.P.) India

http://www.cyberwit.net

Tel: +(91) 9415091004

E-mail: info@cyberwit.net

# CONTENTS

# SOME OTHER WORKS BY GAITHER STEWART

The Fifth Sun, a novel  (Punto Press)

The Trojan Spy, a novel, first volume of the Europe Trilogy (Punto Press)

Lily Pad Roll, a novel, volume two of the Europe Trilogy (Punto Press)

Time of Exile, a novel, volume three of the Europe Trilogy (Punto Press)

Babylon Falling, a collection of essays (Punto Press)

Recollection of Things Learned: Remembering Socialism, essays and articles

(Punto Press)

Signs of the Times, short story collection  (Cyberwit)

Once In Berlin, short story collection  (Wind River Press)

To Be A Stranger, short story collection  (Wind River Press)

Voices From Pisalocca, short story collection  (Kindle e-book by Southern

Cross Review)

Asheville, a novel (Cyberwit)

I

# Acknowledgements

When I proposed the idea of this hybrid book—"hybrid" because composed of both historical non-fiction and a novella of historical fiction — Rowan Wolf, publisher of *Uncommon Thought Journal,* though at first hesitant about the combination of genres, quickly saw its merits, which she explains in her introduction to this volume. In addition to encouragements and suggestions, and besides her introduction here, she also proposed the book title, *Trails of Memory,* which I loved immediately. Rowan Wolf has also posted some of the articles included here on *Uncommon Thought.* Finally, she posted on Internet as a pdf my novella *Words Unspoken,* which constitutes the second half of this book. I am extremely grateful to her for her enormous contribution to *Trails of Memory.*

Secondly, I want to thank Milovana Curuvija in a very special way for her center piece on the back cover of *Trails of Memory* in which in a few words she expresses her own fundamental political stance which coincides with mine. Milovana Curuvija was able to write these succinct words about this book because she had already spent considerable time reading other works by this author which she summed up brilliantly in the limited space on the cover.

I would remember also the assortment of people of forgotten names and nationalities who have passed through my life, men who were in the Battle of Stalingrad, people who have made me love East Europe in general such as the deceased Polish writer Andzei Kusniewicz, an interview with whom appears in this book.

In a particular way I am grateful to both the fictional and non-fictional characters in *Words Unspoken*, the former, who show how they feel about war, the latter, who do what they feel necessary to combat the Nazis who first swept their Germany into the madness of war and who again in the postwar were in control of U.S. occupied Germany which was never denazified as propagandized. Fictional Helmut Seifert Hartmann, who was in the cellars of Stalingrad during the lost battle as a Wehrmacht Intelligence officer in General Paulus' Sixth Army—during which time he never as much as drew his officer's pistol from its holster—was flown out of the encirclement pocket and walked back to the West, making it back to Munich, as he says in the story, like a Galapagos turtle. Aimlessly he went to work for the Nazi-run Gehlen Org in Munich before he finally saw the light, married Ute Friedrich and fled to the Valtellina in Alpine Italy to escape Nazi-CIA clutches and become an anti-Nazi, anti-capitalist journalist in Italy and again in Germany. Helmut is as real to me as those heroic figures of the RAF, the extreme left, underground Red Army Faktion like Ulrike Meinhof, like Gudrun Ensslin who as did Sophie Scholl before them had the courage to declare war on the Nazi state … and paid for it with their lives. I am most fascinated by the ambiguous, bi-cultural Erica-Erika invented by my own imagination; I have never decided whether her Italian or German persona prevailed in her; and I don't know if she too belonged to RAF, if like the others she was arrested by postwar Nazi-run police, and if like the others she also died in a Stammheim prison cell, suicided by the Nazi-run state.

Finally, I want to thank here my friend and computer specialist, Carlo Merlini, for his invaluable technical assistance in the layout and presentation of this book, as well as for some of my past books.

# INTRODUCTION by Rowan Wolf

I did not realize until I read "Trails of Memory – A Century of Nazism" how much that time and political movement has harmonics in this time. I am in the U.S., where decades of effort on the part of one of the major political parties – Republicans – moved them, and perhaps the nation, deeper and deeper to the right. At the same time, the efforts of capitalists continued to break the bonds of community and the treads of continuity, while the broader efforts of Republicans created a more jaded and less informed public. I did know from my studies of white nationalism that it was an ideology that actively spanned continents and was not just contained to North America. Likewise, this movement towards right-wing populism is not confined to the United States, and it is not the only nation experiencing the awful allure of strongman leaders with dreams of dictatorial rule.

Mr. Stewart spoke with me about his idea to write Trails of Memory – A Century of Nazism and merge it with the short stories of Words Unspoken". Being familiar with the latter but not with the former, I thought it sounded like an okay idea. However, I did not have a lot of enthusiasm for the proposal. When Stewart sent me a draft of Trails, I had a much clearer idea of his vision, but more importantly a new insight into Stewart's works of historical fiction. Between his study of history and his own life experiences, he brings life to his stories that truly does make history live again in the lives of "ordinary" people.

Gaither Stewart is an experienced, if unwitting, time traveler and his short stories convey us to the streets and locales of another time. We walk in the shoes of his characters who live in that time. I feel ashamed that I missed this aspect of Stewart's craft. My awareness of my blindness was corrected when I read in his own words and experience the rise of Hitler and the Nazi party, and how the aftermath of that war shaped the lives of millions of people, and the world.

"Trails of Memory – A Century of Nazism" reflects Gaither Stewart's own experience of living in the WWII conflict zones with the people who survived that war. He shares the rise of Hitler and the Nazi party through the eyes of the people rather than those of a politician or the historian. There is a rich mingling of Mr. Stewart's own experience and the experiences of the people he walks among. Just as in a different way we enter the lives of these people in many of his short stories, but most especially in "Words Unspoken".

This dance of historical construction (Trails of Memory) and historical Novel (Words Unspoken) is an excellent read. However, there is a magic here for those who would toss aside history, even historical fiction, as a waste of time in the modern era. I would argue that we have reentered a brave old world as we watch the rise of the dictators and various forms of nationalism. I think we desperately need to understand what we are facing, and where the landmines might well be planted. We need to know how fragile is stability.

One might ask why history is important, though I suspect most readers of this book would never question that premise. For others, the simple answer is "so we don't repeat our mistakes". That answer has been given so often that it is trite and likely many do not pause over what it means to "repeat our mistakes", or for that matter, to repeat our successes. On the individual level when we repeat our mistakes it may bring us pain or frustration. On the collective level our mistakes are amplified geometrically. This points to the difference between "biography" (the individual's story) and history (the collective's experience). History is more than the individual experiences of people added together. The whole is certainly more than the sum of its parts. However, repeating our mistakes – individually or collectively – means that we have not grown. The same is true if we repeat out "successes" over and over again. I hope, and hope that you join me, that over time we become wiser and better versions of ourselves.

This is where works such as this by Gaither Stewart are important. Here, he shares a significant slice of his personal journey and his understanding gained from it, joined together with a fine work of historical fiction. Stewart writes on his perspective of the importance of historical fiction in the Forward of "Words Unspoken." For me, Stewart's words in "Trails of Memory" brought things about the rise of Hitler, and of Nazism to a clarity I had lacked before. It also illuminated some of the events of our current times and challenges. Further, it brought a new appreciation for "Words Unspoken."

My understanding of Hitler and the spread of Nazism across Europe has largely been learned from books. Most American I have known who lived through that had no desire to talk about it, or only about how things were in the U.S. at that time. Most did not have Stewart's experience of an outsider's eyes and a journalist's thirst for the real story living in those places where tanks rolled, bombs dropped, and so many went to their death. Most Americans have little connection to the true losses of war. Maybe that is why we seem to support U.S. military intervention "over there". Not since the Civil War has the U.S. been face to face with those losses. Perhaps that is why so many seem so eager to repeat that war, hoping for a different outcome. That is not the experience of most of the people on the planet who know all too well the horror that war brings.

Given all of that one has to ask why across the world, including where the ugly face of war and nationalism has been experienced, we seem to be rushing into the modern rendition of that era? It is at the worst of times since we are already experiencing the devastation of global warming. This is a time when we need to be seeing ourselves as having a common struggle to pull us together. Instead, we seem to be falling apart at the seams and repeating the worst of our collective mistakes. It also makes these works by Stewart very timely. I believe they can touch you in unexpected ways and bring unexpected insights. It is not too late to turn from the treadmill and step onto the next step of our journey.

# LANDSLIDE INTO NAZISM

Every shadow is in the final analysis a child of light, and only he who experiences light and dark, war and peace, and rise and fall, has truly lived."
(Stefan Zweig: *Die Welt von Gestern)*

In his operatic works the German composer Richard Wagner presented Teutonic gods as "the highest order of beings in the universe". In Wagner's *THE RING*, Wotan, the chief of the gods, who because his power is not absolute resorts to forcefully subjecting others to his will in order to extend his power. Wotan's will to power, the German *Wille zur Macht*, embodies the temptation to use tyranny to achieve full power. Consequentially, although he is aware of the intrinsic dangers of full power, he is simultaneously oppressed by the fear of losing it. In his pathological fear he sets aside morality and natural laws to achieve his personal goals; nonetheless, in the end of his struggle the vestiges of his power slip away and are destroyed and he faces the approach of his doom and the loss of his former glory. The German dictator of the next century, Adolf Hitler, was to idolize Wagner and love his music.

On New Year's Eve of 1918, an unusual winter electrical storm shook the city of Munich marking for Germans the end of the most miserable year since the beginning of the Great War, the great capitalist Civil War called World War One; frightened horses in the stables in the Munich Riding Academy facing the English Garden whinnied in a macabre chorus … some of them old enough to remember the sounds of war in the city on the Isar River. People also feared that the blasts of thunder presaged a long-term downward spiral that would continue unabated in a future time of peace. Though lines of communication were broken and unthinkable things had already happened to them that year, people feared that even worse things were to come about in the new year of 1919. Also that stormy night police sirens whirled out into the city from Leopold Strasse near the university where drunken war profiteers had built street bonfires to celebrate the war's generosity to them. Be that as it may, the rest—dejected, defeated and destitute people alone in the cold of their rooms—observed events with bitterness picturing the hellish festivities going on across the destroyed city, from the Angel of Peace monument hanging ironically from the hill of Bogenhausen to Sendlingertor Platz downtown. Munich people were angry. Time had stripped them of the privileges offered by their homeland. They were angry. They were very angry, the whole people. Germans from the northern seas to the Alps were angry. Angry that their sons and husbands had to die in the trenches of Imperial Germany's war. Angry that many people faced abandoned and alone the poverty of the post-war cold and hunger. And they were angry about the chaos reigning in the government of the emergent so-called Weimar Republic of once mighty Germany.

Mollified somewhat by the historical transformation of the monarchy of the German Empire into a constitutional republic, the populace imagined that the year of 1919 would be the year of the rebirth of a new Germany. Nonetheless, especially young people were confused as to what was right and what was wrong. How could anyone fathom what the dark future held for the wasteland of the post-war Fatherland emanating desolation, melancholy and hopelessness. No place in their beloved land offered certain promises or hopes … no real solace anywhere. What kind of rebirth awaited them? Russians had responded with a revolution. Fundamental change was necessary but the appropriate atmosphere, ambiance and the world view in Germany were wrong. The inflation and the scarcity of necessities caused by war were wrong. Memories of a once great Germany blinked and beckoned, yet eluded the people's grasp; those times were absent and of no use, like something missing and never to return; the present, the black present, reigned supreme. Many people tended to turn their backs and walk away from the past and never look back, passing over the faded footprints of their past of greatness. Many wanted revenge, revenge against the winners in the war;

people wondered who should pay for the devastation of the homeland. How were they to survive in such chaos? Whose fault was the Great War anyway?

Munich intellectuals and university students joined political discussion groups reflecting their personal gripes, their disappointments, their innermost thoughts and their hopes for the future of the nation. People in general clung desperately to the yearning for their lost happiness and those times that seemed lost forever; yet there was wide agreement that Germany should be made great again.

When in November of 1918 the Great War was winding down and the Allies were advancing toward Germany, Germans knew the senseless multi-front war was lost and from north to south, from Berlin to Munich, internal revolution was hatching or already occurring. As a result of the political chaos, when the vilified Kaiser abdicated and the exploitative German nobility abolished, the overly optimistic Social Democrats daringly, conceptually proclaimed Germany a republic with its capital in the small town of Weimar.

Weimar however was just Weimar. It was not the real Germany. For most Germans kept vividly in their mind the remembrance that only a few years earlier their country was the second world economy and its futuristic infrastructures like its railways the envy of the world; they thirsted for the rebirth of that very same Germany. Munich people too continued to dream in a kind of intoxication the highly contagious dream of the return of German greatness and glory—make Germany great again. At the same time, those who understood world realities snickered at the weak, quibbling, humiliating so-called Republic of Weimar. Though Weimar in Central Germany was a city of culture and the home of Wolfgang von Goethe and Friedrich Schiller, the small town was seen as shamefully unfit as the capital of the potential world power that Germany would be again. So widespread was disgust for and opposition to the Weimar political divisions and disabilities—shame and loathing at the very significance of "Weimar"—that disaffected veterans and idle youth joined the proliferating paramilitary organizations like the brutal and well-armed *Freikorps* on the one hand, or discussion groups and action squads of the Communist left on the other. Simultaneously, the German Communist Revolution exploded on the scene in Berlin and Kiel and spread; Rosa Luxemburg and Karl Liebknecht had reformed the Spartacus League, founded the *Die Rote Fahne* (The Red Flag) newspaper and the Communist Party of Germany (KPD). Their declared goal: the destruction of the hated and "guilty" capitalism. Armed workers seized control of train stations, public buildings and the editorial offices of major Berlin newspapers and Liebknecht declared the traitorous Social Democratic (SPD) government deposed.

However, the timing for revolution was wrong, too … and the uprising too late. The SPD and anticommunists—also of the left—with the help of the military establishment had organized the *Freikorps*—the Free Corps, or nationalist militias, made up of war veterans who knew nothing but war and were overjoyed to prolong the fighting. After a week of street fighting, the well-trained *Freikorps* settled the issue by killing the Communist leaders Rosa Luxemburg and Karl Liebknecht. By January 11, 1919 the revolution was crushed and many revolutionaries dead.

A *de facto* republic since the preceding November, by February 1919 when a national assembly meeting in Weimar adapted a Constitution, Germany became a *de jure* republic. In its fourteen years of existence, the Weimar Republic faced the enormous economic and political problems of hyperinflation, the political extremism of left and right paramilitaries, and contentious relationships with the intimidating victors in the Great War. Resentment towards the Versailles Treaty was strong especially on the political right; rightists were not reconciled with the peace treaty and they hated both the signatories and those Germans who tried to fulfill its terms. Nonetheless, though the Weimar Republic did fulfill most of the terms of Versailles, it never met its disarmament requirements—the *Freikorps* were a subterfuge—and paid only a small portion of the war reparations. Moreover, though Weimar Germany accepted the western borders of the country, it too disputed the eastern borders such as those with Austria and the Sudetenland assigned by Versailles to Czechoslovakia.

During the confusing year of 1919, Munich University was practically shut down. Lectures were sporadic. Students and city people could only observe the turbulence, the confusion and the disorder happening in Munich and in their country that by its very nature demanded order. Mean and incomprehensible things were occurring, greed and misery rampant. In that chaotic atmosphere groups of young men in brand new brown uniforms began appearing in public, marching in small groups or sitting orderly on the rear platforms of new troop trucks. Communists? *Reichswehr*, the regular German Army? No one knew for certain. They looked different. Whose were they? Who financed them? Big industrialists, one said. Maybe foreigners. How did they fit into the picture average people saw?

Müncheners are beer drinkers. Bavarians love the multi-storied establishments of each of Munich's major breweries with their restaurants and meeting halls: the Löwenbräukeller, the Paulanerbräu and the Hofbräuhaus and others. In those times when poverty stricken men sat whole days in a beer hall nursing one liter of beer, they unwittingly observed history in the making: the debut of a new European political figure. The new man on the scene, Adolf Hitler, made his name as a popular speaker in Munich beer halls.

Meanwhile, confusing things were occurring all over Germany. In Bavaria disparate historical events were crowded into brief, breathless periods of time. When in November 1918 King Ludwig of Bavaria abdicated, a politician named Kurt Eisner, the leader of the Independent Social Democratic Party of Germany, became Minister-President of Bavaria and declared it a People's State. Though Eisner advocated a socialist republic he distanced his party from Russian Bolsheviks, guaranteed private property and was totally unable to provide public services. So that in the January 1919 Bavarian elections he was defeated, and reflecting the unpredictability of the times and the fickleness of the people, Eisner was assassinated in February by a right-wing nationalist, Count Anton von Arco-Valley. Surprisingly, for a short time the people of Bavaria *were* more leftist—though less so than believed as Kurt Eisner's fate had shown. Even though the Social Democrats were widely hated, it was still a surprise when two months later in April, 1919, as Communist revolution continued to spread throughout Germany, the Bavarian Soviet Republic was established in Munich: *Räterepublik Baiern*—a largely conceptual Bavarian Soviet Republic. During the revolution in Berlin and Munich, many other sub-states of the Deutsches Reich—the German Empire—harbored the same secessionist desires as did stolid separatist Bavaria. Still, when a month after the Bavarian Soviet Republic demanded independence from the Weimar Republic, it was immediately smashed to smithereens by the German Army and the paramilitary *Freikorps;* thousands of persons were arrested and jailed at Munich's Stadelheim Prison, many of whom were executed.

I am not a historian but I am an avid reader of history. I feel obligated to underline that although I am not even tempted to try to write history as such, I am writing *about* a certain history. While recounting the history recorded by others I have concentrated on the snippets, the bits and pieces of history some of which I have personally experienced, either directly or indirectly. Bavaria, where Nazism as we know it today was born, is a case in point. One war after Hitler, I lived among Bavarians for a long period, studied in the university in Munich, began journalism there and lived in a Bavarian village south of the city where my children attended the village school and spoke Bavarian dialect. So I can say with a non-historian's sincerity that I do know Bavarians ... admittedly to a certain extent—for how well do we ever know other peoples? I found that Bavarians are truly different from other Germans. Their dialect is unlike anything in the rest of Germany, the thickest of which is incomprehensible to the "Prussian pigs" as they refer in jest to northern Germans or sometimes to non-Bavarians in general. Bavarians are independent-minded but not revolutionary, curious but vacillating, fickle and capricious. They are conservative and progressive at the same time. They listen, and then decide. Unfortunately, they listened to the Austrian Adolf Schicklgruber who would become Adolf Hitler dictator of Germany; they liked his message but though he spoke their same Bavarian language they did not understand his real intentions and the extent of his unlimited ambitions. It seems that one century ago no one imagined the profundity of the rocky abyss into which the man named Schicklgruber would lead Munich, Germany, Europe, the world.

In hindsight, it seems that by 1922 more observers of Adolf Hitler (born in Braunau am Inn in 1889, only 121 kilometers east of Munich) should have been aware that fire lay under the embers of his messages in that post-war world. They could have suspected that Adolf Hitler was leading Germany and Europe into a dark tunnel at the end of which lay total tragedy. And that the price would be much higher than that paid for the more limited imperialism of the Kaiser. But in fact even the most politically astute seemed blind to the dimensions of the danger Hitler posed already in those early years—in the years before the landslide—a blindness that reflected the confusion and the chaos in the whole of Germany headed in a direction from which there was no return. The mad folly that infected not only Germany and Germanized East Europe—the Prussian Kaiser's *Mitteleuropa*— but the world. Nobel writer Heinrich Böll's "Buffalo" (Hitler) was upon the German people, unshakable and irremovable in his mad attempt to conquer the world or pull it down with him into that waiting abyss. Post-war inflation and defeatism were not the ultimate decisive threats to the future Germany, nor was Internationalist Communism the major threat to a normal Germany; rabid nationalism led by a madman riddled by dreams, legend and the will to power was the lethal threat ... and his message of militarism and revanchism and totalitarianism and insane anti-Semitism.

Although those historical events occurred long before our times of today, I lived the years after World War Two in the same places as did Adolf Hitler after World War One. I lived there in times that only seem vastly different from the times I am describing. That is not the case. Times and events since Hitler's demise had proceeded orderly, however dialectically, one thing leading to its opposite in my times—post-World War Two as in post-World War One. As a student at Munich University I perceived in my German friends and acquaintances the same sense of hopelessness that follows war and destruction. And I encountered in the Munich student and youth world a sense of shame and of vindication for what had been perpetrated by their own government in their name against peoples of East and West. At the same time, people again wanted to forget that past. Those memories caused both rage and anguish, torment and hate. And that past was fixed and unchangeable. With time and a powerful enough will Germans might have been able to create a new future but that toxic past was ineradicable. In my times I also perceived a growing resentment against the winners of the war, this time not only exploiters but also occupiers. I perceived the emergence of a new internationalist and leftist generation in Germany in contrast to the nationalistic racist revanchist generation of their fathers. That generation too has been smothered and nearly silenced by NATO and the European Union.

In March 1918 the extreme nationalist, Anton Drexler, founded the party that was to become the German Workers' Party (*Deutsche Arbeiter Partei*, DAP). The new man on the scene, an Austrian serving by special dispensation in the German Army, personified the magical key that unlocked a new form of nationalism. Adolf Schicklgruber's first DAP speech was held in Munich's famous Hofbräukeller on October 16, 1919, where he spoke before one hundred and eleven people, some of whom were likely curious beer-drinkers from the Munich hinterland. A vain person and conscious of his ability to sway others, Hitler himself later uninhibitedly declared that was the day when he realized he could really "make a good speech". At first, Hitler's speeches sounded as a faint whisper in the dark, looming up like an echo out of the distant past, like a magical tune or a memory coming from obscure northern forests; yet if one heard well, his words revealed old passions and resounded the rhythms of ancient prejudices and undying hates which identified him as both the charmer of peoples and the murderer of whole races that he was to become. At first, Adolf Schicklgruber-Hitler spoke to relatively small groups, but his considerable oratorical and propaganda skills were appreciated by the still uncertain party leadership. While formally a lance-corporal in the German Army and not even a German yet, in early 1920 the Austrian, Adolf Schicklgruber-Hitler, became the party propaganda chief. His magnetism and his words that many wanted to hear began to make the party more public. On 24 February 1920, he organized the party's biggest meeting yet of two thousand people in the *Staatliches Hofbräuhaus*, Munich's most famous beer hall. And the time counter to landslide was already ticking. It was in this speech that Hitler enunciated the twenty-five points of the German Workers' Party manifesto, giving the organization a bold stratagem with a clear foreign policy: abrogation of the Treaty of Versailles, a Greater Germany, Eastern expansion and exclusion of Jews from citizenship. The manifesto was clearly anti-Semitic, anti-capitalist, anti-democratic, anti-Marxist and anti-liberal. Yet foreign capitalist investors stood in line to iron out agreements to pour funds into Hitler's coffers and into his pockets.

On the same day of Hitler's Hofbräuhaus speech the DAP changed its name to the *Nationalsozialistische Deutsche Arbeiterpartei* ("National Socialist German Workers' Party" or Nazi Party). Over Hitler's objections the word *Socialist* was added by the party's executive committee in order to appeal to left-wing workers ... one of the last decisions not made or approved by the emerging leader. After that success, Hitler began lecturing in various Munich beer halls, meetings attended by a growing number of intellectuals and students whom the party courted. And Hitler—who could make a good speech—was the main attraction.

In that same February of 1921 a small "hall protection" was organized, which by autumn of that year was called *Sturmabteilung* (Storm Detachment), or SA. But it was Hitler who drew the crowds. So it was that by the end of that year Nazi party members numbered two thousand. But the Party (NSDAP) organization recognized that without Hitler the party was dead; reluctantly—or perhaps not at all—the old party leadership granted him full powers and made him party chairman. During 1922 and 1923 Hitler's Nazi Party created two more organizations that would come to have great significance: the *Hitler Youth* and a guard unit that eventually became *Schutzstafel,* the dreaded SS. With these organizations behind him, Hitler—inspired by Mussolini's March on Rome in 1922—decided that coup d'ètat was the right strategy to seize control of Germany. Hitler loyal elements within the German Army had helped the SA Brown Shirts procure barracks and modern weapons, but the march order never arrived because Hitler was arrested, tried and sentenced to prison for a failed beer hall putsch. Pardoned a year later, Hitler— a man in a hurry as are most tyrants on their way up—used the time in a Bavarian jail to dictate to his deputy Rudolf Hess the first volume of his book, *Mein Kampf.*

Most likely because of the reality that even he could be jailed, Herr Hitler, now the undisputed leader, *Der Führer,* changed his mind and decided that power was to be achieved not through revolution but by legal means. In Germany's federal elections in December 1924 the new NAZI Party garnered 6.6% of the vote, 1,918, 329 voters. From then on it was a gradual but unstoppable march to power in 1933. Adolf Hitler knew the German people; he knew the thinking of the German people better than they themselves. He knew their anger. And he knew their inherent need for order. *Ordnung muss sein*!

Stefan Zweig underlines a counterview that since Germany has ALWAYS been a class society, many Germans did not take seriously a leader who had never finished elementary school and moreover made his name in Munich beer halls. Such a person could not be the leader of the great German people. Even when Adolf Hitler was named Chancellor in 1933, the public was convinced it was only a temporary arrangement and that German *Ordnung* would soon return and a properly educated person of the leadership class would assume power. In those times, however,

*Ordnung* on a national scale was more important than freedom and law. Zweig recalls Goethe saying that disorder was worse than even lawlessness. 'Everything is in order'—*Alles ist in Ordnung* is an important expression in the German language.

Hitler also understood the willingness of the Allies to believe any promises that furthered peace. People of the world refused to believe the unbelievable that was soon upon them. Hitler's intuition about the mentalities of Germans and the Allies was right; he garnered much help from outside his own party and his own organizations: Kaiser-true Monarchists and the Wittelsbach monarchs in Munich considered Hitler their man; Nationalists believed he was preparing the road to power and glory for them; heavy industry and the capitalist USA considered Hitler—whom they had been supporting for years—as protection against Bolshevism; the petite bourgeoisie saw him as a savior. Social Democrats did not oppose him either because they saw in him a dreamlike opportunity, the nemesis of their arch enemies, the Communists.

Moreover, the Left had been neutralized in such a way that there continued to be bad blood between the Communist Party (KPD) and the Socialist Party (SPD) which prevented them from working together—contrary to orders from Moscow to the Communists. The KPD justly portrayed the SPD as the primary bourgeois threat to socialism in Germany. That rivalry between Communists and Socialist Democrats which proved to be permanent, not transitory—Communists considered the Socialists as betrayers of the Revolution and the Socialists saw the Communists as puppets of Moscow—rebounded to the advantage of the Nazi Party: only a parliamentary coalition of the KPD and SPD could have prevented the Nazis from coming to power. Even at the height of their influence in the *Reichstag*, the Nazis never had sufficient delegates to resist such a coalition.

While Hitler unabashedly promised something to everyone, the most varied political parties considered him their friend. Not even rich German Jewry understood the bitter reality of what was rapidly coming to a head. Many Jews believed the

German state apparatus and its holy Constitution were morally better than they were. Rich assimilated Jews faced a never resolved quandary: they wanted to retain their Jewishness but they did not want to admit it either. They could never do what was necessary to achieve the aspired Germanhood. As we will see, both Walter Benjamin and Kafka wrote extensively on that fundamental problem of German Jewry.

Then there was the touchy question of foreign aid, especially from the USA. When did it begin? How much did it count in the successes of Nazism? How much responsibility does it bear for the evil and destruction Nazism provoked? In 1921 the Allied Reparation Commission set the final German reparations bill at 132 billion gold marks, as usual the victors dictating the settlement and thus the history of the "Great War" and its aftermath ... and also the not too distant future. When Germany defaulted in January 1932, France and Belgium occupied the Ruhr in order to force repayment ... but that act backfired and strengthened German revanchism. Germans reacted with a government-sponsored campaign of passive resistance while the German economy itself spiraled into hyperinflation. German currency collapsed and wagon loads of marks were necessary to buy a loaf of bread. Although the Nazi Party program called for nationalization, the privatization introduced in the mid-1930s was to benefit the wealthiest sectors in order to gain their political support and to stimulate foreign investments. It worked quite well. Leading industrialists at home like I.G. Farben and foreign investors from the USA, Great Britain, France and Sweden supported the Nazi Party and Hitler's ascension to power, in exchange for which Hitler privatized a great number of state monopolies. The League of Nations and other international organizations took note and foreign investors saw a bonanza in Germany. Fresh money flowed into German coffers while Germany re-armed. One important result of the reparations agreement was Germany's re-occupation of its Ruhr region—the Rhineland—the industrial heart of Germany.

Since 1930, Germany's "beloved" President Hindenburg had backed the long established class Chancellorship but the Great Depression, exacerbated by government policies of deflation, caused a surge in unemployment and like other countries Germany was bankrupt, with the result that in 1933 Hindenburg appointed Adolf Hitler as Chancellor with the Nazi Party as part of a coalition government. Within months, the infamous Reichstag fire—the burning of the Parliament building in Berlin—and the *Enabling Act* that gave Hitler wide powers wiped out constitutional governance and civil liberties. Hitler's "legal" seizure of power meant government by decree without legislative participation. The republic ended, democracy collapsed and a single-party state and the dictatorship of the Nazi era began. And before long oppositional and undesirable persons were being interned in the first Nazi concentration camp in Dachau near Munich. By the time of the outbreak of war in 1939, Nazi Party membership was necessary to get and keep jobs such as university professor. In the same fateful year of 1933 when Hitler acquired full powers, the statesman  and according to writer Saul Bellow a kind of "elective king",  Franklin D. Roosevelt, came to power in the United States of America—at the time a lukewarm pro-Soviet Union  power center—while concomitant  with popular Rooseveltism, both Communism and Nazism/Fascism spread in the depression-plagued schizophrenic USA. The world would no longer be the same.

As a student at Munich University in the late 1960s I perceived in my acquaintances the sense of hopelessness that follows war. And I saw in the Munich student world shame and a desire for vindication for what had been perpetrated by their own government against peoples of East and West: anyone over fifty was suspect of participation in the tragedy. The tragic past that just as after World War One many people wanted to forget … but couldn't. The stain lay too deep. The defeat was too terrible. It would take decades to overcome the guilt complex of a people. I also perceived widespread resentment against the self-proclaimed Allied victors of WW Two, this time seen by youth as exploiters and occupiers. The Korean and Vietnam wars seemed to them confirmation of their suspicions of the victors. I witnessed also the emergence of a new internationalist leftist generation in Germany in contrast to the nationalistic racist revanchist generation of their fathers born after the Great War. That new leftist generation also inevitably turned to violence as we will see in the Baader-Meinhof Group/ Rote Armee Faktion. However, today, leftists of their quality seldom show their faces in Germany, in the West. *Gleichschaltung* (the Nazi "synchronization" or the total conformity of each individual and every aspect of life) still exists in what is politically and socially correct in the everyday life of our times.

Heinrich Böll (1917-1985), Nobel for literature in 1972, is one of my favorite writers; I consider him one of the most worthy among Nobel Literary Prize winners. Born in Cologne, he grew up in the Nazi period, refused to join the Hitler Youth but as a soldier in World War Two was wounded four times. His major work, *Billiards At Half-past Nine*, tells a story of three generations of one family and their relation to power in a Germany ruled over by "The Buffalo" in the novel in reference to President Hindenburg but in reality symbolizing Hitler and Nazism. In their policy of "synchronization and harmonization" of society, the *Gleichschaltung* demanded by Nazism in power, persons who partake of "the host of the beast" (Nazism) brainwash and oppress those of the "host of the lamb", those for whom the human factor still counted, while however the old continental illness of Eurocentrism  not only survived the great European slaughter of the Great War but centered on the ideological struggle  between Fascism and Communism, a sort of transhistorical battle over the very soul of man, seemingly transcending and ignoring the complexities of the underlying immediate social needs of the individual in whose everyday life it was everyman for himself. No book tells it better than Böll's. Few others have demonstrated more dramatically the dangers of "partaking of the host of the Buffalo".

Also an American writer expressed the same dismay at the events happening in Germany. After a visit to Nazi Germany, the Asheville writer, Thomas Wolfe, published a story in *The New Republic* entitled, *I Have a Thing to Tell You.* Wolfe paid a high price for that story: his books would be banned in Germany and he would never again be able to visit the country he loved. The story of a few months after he returned to America from Nazi Germany is a powerful piece that concludes with a touching good-bye. "To that old German land with all the measure of its truth, its glory, beauty, magic and its ruin," Wolfe wrote, "to that dark land, to that old ancient earth that I have loved so long—I said farewell."

Yet, even in this tyrannical system of enforced total synchronization, there were exceptions who never partook of the host of the beast, who never believed, but as a rule the price they paid was high. Some chose exile abroad; but some rejected Nazism and stayed and resisted.

# THE FINAL DAYS

## Sophie Scholl Rebels In Munich

Over and over again history repeats itself. We know the histories of world wars, the Great War or World War One and then its echo, World War Two. We see "false flag operations" and "regime change" plots over and over again. Those who think that history does not repeat itself might read these lines about what happened in Munich during the Nazi era and in light of what is happening today in the world conclude it is all happening again. After World War II the area with the great fountain in front of Munich's Ludwig-Maximilian University (LMU) on the famed Ludwig Strasse was named the Geschwister Scholl Platz in honor of the anti-Nazi brother and sister Scholl who in 1943 led the student *White Rose* resistance movement against the Nazi dictatorship. In the main building of the university—in which I studied—not so many years earlier Sophie and Hans Scholl had distributed anti-regime leaflets and paid for that "crime" with their lives.

In the best known film about the Scholl siblings, *The Final Days*, (2005) Sophie  Scholl joins the White Rose student organization run by her brother Hans. They have prepared copies of their sixth anti-Nazi leaflet which Sophie and Hans stack outside university lecture rooms. With only minutes left before the end of the class period, Sophie goes to the top floor and pushes the remaining copies over the balustrade. As Hans and Sophie are leaving, a janitor who saw Sophie scatter the leaflets holds them until police arrive and arrest them. The siblings are taken to the Munich Stadelheim Prison and interrogated by the Gestapo. Initially Sophie claims she and Hans had nothing to do with the fliers; she just noticed them in the hall and pushed a stack off the railing because it is in her nature to play pranks. She is about to be dismissed when the order arrives to hold her. The investigation has incontrovertible evidence that Sophie and Hans were responsible for the distribution of anti-Nazi leaflets. Sophie concedes her involvement (as does Hans) but determined to protect the others she maintains that the production and distribution of the leaflets in cities throughout the region were entirely the work of her brother and herself. Sophie argues that before the 1933 Nazi take-over the freedom of speech was guaranteed by law. She describes atrocities committed by the Nazis including reports of concentration camps related by soldiers returning fro the Eastern front. She assumes all blame and refuses to name accomplices. Sophie, her brother and a married friend with three children, Christoph Probst, are charged with treason, troop demoralization and abetting the enemy. In a show trial they are condemned to death. Sophie declares that many people agree with what she and her group have said and written, but they dare not express such thoughts. She has the courage to tell the court that "where we stand today, you will stand soon." That same day Sophie is guillotined. The blade falls and the picture goes black. Footsteps are heard, then Hans's voice exclaims "*Es lebe die Freiheit*!" ("Long live Freedom!"), before the blade falls again. Probst is brought in next and the blade falls once more. In the closing shot, thousands of leaflets fall from the sky over Munich. A title explains that copies of the White Rose manifesto were smuggled to Scandinavia and then to England, where the Allies printed millions of copies of the "Manifesto of the Students of Munich" that were subsequently dropped on German cities. The first frames of the credits list the names of the seven members of the White Rose group who were executed, more than a dozen who were imprisoned, and supporters and sympathizers who received draconian punishments. Fearful of an opposition movement rooted among youth across the nation, Gestapo interrogators asked the Scholls about the reasons for and significance of the name, The White Rose. So as not to furnish police any leads, Hans allegedly claimed he chose the name simply because it sounded good.

The Scholls were born and grew up the small town of Forchtenberg in the southern German state of Baden-Württemberg , Sophie in 1921, children of the politically active, anti-Nazi Mayor of Forchtenberg, Robert Scholl, who was jailed twice during the Nazi reign, four months the first time for calling Hitler, "the scourge of God", and after Hans and Sophie's execution to eighteen months for "listening to enemy broadcasts". To his disgust his children joined the Hitler Youth in which Sophie was active and became a leader, until finally Robert dissuaded them and they too began seeing the realities of what was happening in Germany. By the time they left home for studies at Munich University they had made other political choices. At war's end Robert Scholl became Mayor of the city of Ulm 156 kilometers west of Munich and in 1952 was a co-founder of the All-German People's Party.

Robert Scholl himself was a curious figure who occupied ambivalent positions of many non-Nazis in post-war Germany. The Gesamtdeutsche Volkspartei was a center-left, pacifist party of dissidents from the Christian Democratic Union (CDU) who disagreed with Chancellor Konrad Adenauer's American-imposed foreign and intra-German policies; it opposed German re-armament and militarization and integration into NATO as impediments to the reunification of East and West Germany. The phantom of divide and conquer already in the 1950s haunted NATO controlled-Europe, with U.S. forces occupying and controlling Germany and Italy and the top secret Gladio organization gearing up to tighten American reins on all of West Europe.

Twenty-five years later during student rebellions across the Western world, Sophie and Hans Scholl in Munich were remembered. They had become symbols of resistance … another reminder that history does indeed repeat itself. Sophie would say that courage has always been the ultimate question for each of us. Knowledge requires courage. Again today, in another place and time, I have recalled the Scholls. A few years ago I kept a log of manifestations of Fascistic violence throughout Italy, echoing the way Nazism began in the 1920s in Germany, and now is being repeated in many places in the world.

*December 6, 2017: Fascists-Nazis are on the attack across all of Italy. Today Nazi-Fascist demonstrations in front of the offices of the Liberal La Repubblica, one of Europe's major newspapers, and the leftist Espresso weekly magazine, both in Rome. "We're here to stay, they announce. "No truce now." and they are strong throughout the country. Masked faces, fire bombs in the center of Rome. Fascists-Nazis! No holds barred.*

*December 7, 2017: militants of Fascist Forza Nuova (New Force) are rampaging throughout Italy. After yesterday's demonstrations at the newspaper, La Repubblica and left-wing weekly Espresso, handmade bombs were planted early this morning in front of a Carabiniere station on Rome's central Piazza San Giovanni. At the same time the press is reporting on extensive million Euro financial dealings of Forza Nuova (FN) in Kiev, Ukraine and in Crimea. These are dangerous signals of the growing Fascist menace and financial maneuvers to support it. Let no one think spreading Fascism in Europe or the USA is merely sensationalistic journalism. It started this way for Hitler in Munich and Mussolini in Rome. The Nazi government in Ukraine is becoming a symbol. The history of Fascism is being repeated.*

*December 8, 2017: in the city of Forli in eastern Italy, Fascists armed with clubs clashed with anti-Fascists; a member of the left-wing metal workers trade union was injured. In Como in north Italy, anti-Fascists marched in protest against Fascism and intolerance. In Naples, Fascists slogans were found in front of the local offices of La Repubblica newspaper. Meanwhile a Demos Poll shows that 46% of the Italian electorate is worried about violence by Fascist extremists.*

*December 10, 2017: militants of Forza Nuova and anti-Fascists clashed on the streets of a cold Milan, the capital of north Italy, clashes squashed then by police anti-riot forces. The tam tam of the social networks got many anti-fascists on the streets in record time and the Fascists got the worst of the conflict this time. THIS time. Today the Fascist Party is Italy's second political party. The*

Every day historical evils are repeated. And it does not require courage to become aware of the evils happening around us. The Scholls show that courage is however required to do something about those evils. Before arriving in Munich I had witnessed the first stirrings among the student population in Berkeley in the 1960s. I admired the fiery orators, and imagined emulating them. I marveled at their awareness and interpretations of world events.

Then in Munich I began reading Lenin and Marx more seriously, more personally, studies which eventually changed my world outlook. I had trouble grasping the historical difficulty of synchronizing European Socialism with Russian Communism and the significance of the concept of *revolution*. Not that I believed then in the possibility of the resurgence of Nazism: Hitler was dead and gone forever but I did not yet realize that the ballyhooed denazification in Germany never took place. Instead the U.S. government had enlisted German Nazis in its war against the Soviet Union and had assisted literally countless top Nazis to escape to Latin America and elsewhere via "ratlines" organized by the CIA, the Vatican and various complicit governments and institutions. Still, the times of revolution in Europe seemed over and done, and I accepted assurances that the history of Nazism could not repeat itself. On the other hand, it became clearer each day that Germany was an instrument of American power—not an ally but a vassal and an occupied country. I witnessed it happening; authority in new Germany was infested with ex-Nazis. In 1967 the war in Vietnam was raging, over a half- million US soldiers were there and the yearly military draft of young Americans growing. In that period German youth looked at everyone over forty with suspicion. Nazi! Fascist! Murderer!

Some 400,000 Nazis, former active party members were held in internment camps from 1945-45 and were gradually tried by a Denazification Tribunal with the official task of convicting those guilty of war crimes and keeping Nazis out of positions of power and influence in the new Germany. Procedures however were lukewarm and lenient because precisely German Nazis were of help to Western powers, especially the USA … above all in the Cold War. The U.S. had few East European experts; German Nazi specialists were many. Nazis began occupying also political positions in the West German government in Bonn: the former high-ranking Nazi, Kurt Georg Kiesinger, who led the Federal Republic of Germany from 1966-69, is a prime example. Kiesinger had joined the Nazi Party in 1933 and held important positions in the Foreign Affairs Ministry. Thirty years later in the post-war little changed for him in the Federal Republic of Germany, the FRG. After a laughable denazification procedure he joined the ruling Christian Democratic Party instead of the NSDAP, held a job in the defense and security sector instead of Nazi foreign affairs, became Vice-President of the European Council, and finally got the top job: Chancellor—the same position occupied by Hitler in the Nazi state—and all the while most certainly controlled by and working hand in glove with the CIA running the new state of Germany. The whole denazification effort was abandoned in 1951. Former Nazi Party members were everywhere. The USA had lost all interest in the denazification program; the British handed over the management of the panels to the Germans themselves who anyway detested the program; and the French ran the mildest possible denazification effort of all. Only in Soviet controlled East Germany, the DDR, was denazification considered a critical element of the transformation into a socialist society and was stricter in its opposition to Nazism than in the West.

An American academic friend in Munich, Jack Aigler, Professor of European History at the Munich branch of University of Maryland in the 60s and 70s, was obsessed with the imminent recrudescence of Nazi Germany. For him it was a socio-political certainty, its ideology inherent in the German people, only superficially cloaked by America's hypocritical democratization of the defeated enemy as a consequence of the exigencies of the Cold War. "We wanted anticommunist allies in Central Europe," he pontificated to his students those evenings I sat in on his class, "Well, we've got them. We've got a tiger by the tail. Let's arm them all and give them the green light. Then we'll have a real bulwark against Bolshevism," he said. This feeling was linked to the story that circulated among Germans: why hadn't America united with Germany and whipped the Russians? Many recall that persons like two-gun General Patton considered the alliance of America and Germany without Hitler the natural order of things. According to Professor Aigler, America and the ex-Nazis got their wish. Not that my friend Jack was a leftist ahead of his times, but he saw aspects of the Cold War which I did not yet grasp. "An iron bastion against the Commies! Hah! You see all those gray Bundeswehr uniforms around town!" he warned repeatedly. "And everywhere you hear *Deutschland Deutschland über alles*. Just wait till the Nazis take over again. Then we'll see the tail wagging Europe. They're too powerful a people; their instincts and their destiny are for expansion." For him Munich's Föhn winds that he hid from symbolized the threat of renascent Nazism. When the Nazi-Föhn winds blew down from the Alps he sealed his apartment with hermetic shutters so that night reigned there constantly. He said the malefic Föhn had the same effect on people as Nazism. On such days when surgeons refused to operate and mechanics wouldn't adjust a carburetor and judges refused to judge, Jack locked himself in, dressed in a long robe and red silk scarf high around his neck, wore heavy sunglasses over steel-rimmed eye glasses, plunged rubber plugs in his ears that he boasted reached to his eardrums and passed the day drinking Pernod. The wind that departs quietly from the Sahara, whips across the Mediterranean and serpentines through the Alps and descends on the plains of Bavaria like the arm of capricious Fate was for Jack a physical enemy, inimical and inexorable, to be combated with all possible weapons. He needed the Föhn-Nazism, and spared nothing to defend all of us with the Pernod he bought by the case at the PX.

University students in Munich became infused with the ardor that eventually blossomed into revolutionary 1968 and gave birth to the terrorist Red Army Faktion, known as the Baader-Meinhoff Gang. Hans and Sophie Scholl had been beheaded only a little over a decade earlier. *Die Weisse Rose*, the White Rose, might live again.

One precise historical precedent to the 1967-68 student revolt in Munich was remembered by some young people aiming at remaking society: on November 7, 1918 Munich workers led by the bearded Berlin journalist, pure-of-purpose Kurt Eisner had staged a socialist revolution—local and more or less spontaneously—and people discussed the role of "good intentions"—that only good could flow from good—and the eventual emergence of the ideal political leader. It was still disconcerting to me that Eisner's politics was bloody business. For Eisner's revolutionary regime—in the words of Max Weber 'run by poets, semi-poets, mezzo-philosophers and schoolteachers'—left a trail of blood and violence behind it. There is a place in Munich's Müller Strasse where the Workers Regime executed a certain Countess Westarp and nine hostages. At some point in those years I read the Brecht quote: *Welche Niedrichkeit würdest Du nicht begehen um die Niedrigkeit abzuschlagen?* Eisner's subsequent electoral defeat and assassination by the anti-Semitic Bavarian aristocrat, Count Anton von Arco-Valley, in April of the next year led to a bloody military repression of the "Socialist" participants in Catholic Bavaria's only political deviation to the left: in the cellar in the St. Georg Palais the reactionary White Guard shot twenty-one youths of the St. Joseph Gesellenverein. Bavaria was then ripe to become the seedbed of the National Socialism of Adolph Hitler.

From that history I learned that "spontaneous revolution" was not real revolution; at the most it may be one of the first stages of the process of revolution. History shows that spontaneous uprisings and revolts alone lead to repression, reaction and the crushing of the revolutionary spirit for long periods afterwards. For what kind of a revolution could a *Saupreussen* journalist—a Prussian pig as real Müncheners called Northerners—organize among unorganized Munich workers who in 1918 were just hungry and destitute at war's end, while even the revolt of the Communist Spartacists led by Karl Liebknecht and Rosa Luxemburg, with a real party and the best leftist leaders of Germany, was failing in Berlin.

Historians like to pose terrifying "what if questions". Since Eisner's 'purity of purpose' conviction instead of engendering good, willy-nilly paved the way for evil, the question here is again spontaneity and chance: What if Eisner had not left Berlin for Munich? Would there still have been that short-lived Bavarian Socialist State? And if not, would another Adolf Hitler still have been welcomed in aristocratic Catholic Bavaria to march with his men down Ludwig Strasse past Munich's great university? And would the history of twentieth century Europe have been different?

Busy as we were in the 1970s with the festive side of Munich, Oktoberfest and Carnival parties, my friends and I didn't often discuss political subjects like Capitalism and Socialism. Yet my own past in the American South seemed dead and sometimes I heard a summons, like a call to the future, a future that weighed on my past. I began to wonder about that past: if instead I had been born German in the post-WWI period, I too might have fought for the same ideals as Sophie and Hans Scholl; or, like Brecht I too might have committed 'any vileness in order to eliminate vileness'. Or, I came to realize, if I had been born German of an earlier generation I could have been together with Rosa Luxemburg—or perhaps by a twist of destiny become a National Socialist Nazi.

Time and place are truly mysteries. Everything seems to be circles and repetitions. And chance. Subjects and objects. Who decides which is which? Who decides such things? Who brings a Hitler to Munich? How and why do people like Hans and Sophie Scholl emerge from the morass? Is that truly all chance? For as

Sophie said in her final words: they wanted to regain their past ... the past when the law guaranteed freedom of speech. Their image of the past seems to us reconstructed. Personal. Distinct. And you realize that the past is always incomplete. And that history is people. So what about the personal courage she displayed? Though interesting, history cannot account for it ... nor can it account for cowardice, either. So the closest to truth might be our own perceptions and interpretations of what we think might have happened ... which is not reality ... perhaps not even close to what really happened.

There are times when each single event seems absolute. Eisner was in Munich. Rosa Luxemburg was in Berlin. Yet in the unfolding of events nothing is absolute, for sundry things are linked and go on changing, fundamentally, and from one moment to the next you come to the realization that history is repeating itself. So you come to believe less and less in absolutes. You learn to mistrust absolutists who demand specific answers, who demand yes or no, who prefer white to black, this to that, and use expressions like 'in the final analysis'.

It seems I seldom understand what is happening to me while it is happening. And I'm nervous and unclear about what exactly is going on in my world today. But I believe if you open your eyes and begin to really see, you understand that so many things alien to yourself  but which act on you are ambiguous, ambivalent, two-edged and paradoxical. One says that is life. Still, I'm conscious of the helplessness and insignificance you feel when you are unable to see what it is you yourself are doing. It is a lonely feeling. Is it the same quagmire with others? I've hated to choose; as if I knew the correct answers and the right choices. I can only guess. I like to think I might have some minimal influence on events—maybe as much as one grain of sand influences the level of the sea. And even if I could exert any influence it might cause damage as political and military leaders prove day by day.

However, in lonely sleepless nights you might wonder about your own courage. In such moments you might ask yourself: Would I have Sophie's courage? You wonder if heroes like the Scholls are born or created by circumstances. Courage! The necessary quality—right and just—to awaken awareness of injustice and create dissent. The dissent that can then create the awareness that resistance is the next step … the step toward rebellion and finally revolution.

Throughout history heroines like Sophie Scholl have emerged and stepped onto center stage. In the name of justice they have challenged Power with demands for normal rights even though established Power labels those demands treason. But always they challenge Power: Antigone, Joan of Arc, Anne Frank and Sophie Scholl.

The question Sophie asked herself was how the individual must act under a dictatorship. She and members of The White Rose instructed Germans to passively resist the Nazi government. The pamphlet used Biblical and philosophical support for an intellectual argument about resistance. In addition to authorship, Sophie helped copy and distribute pamphlets while also managing the group's finances. She and the rest of the White Rose were arrested for distributing that sixth leaflet at Munich University on 18 February 18, 1943. In the People's Court on February 22, 1943, Sophie Scholl was recorded as saying these words:

*"Somebody, after all, had to make a start. What we wrote and said is also believed by many others. They just don't dare express themselves as we did."*

Else Gebel who shared Sophie Scholl's cell recorded her last words before being taken away to be executed: *"It is such a splendid sunny day, and I have to go …. What does my death matter if by our acts thousands are warned and alerted? Among the student body there will certainly be a revolt."*

In a historical context, the White Rose's legacy has had significance for many commentators and artists as a demonstration of personal courage and as a well-documented case of social dissidence in a society of violent repression, censorship and conformist pressure. Playwright Lillian Garrett-Groag stated in *Newsday* on February 22, 1993, that "It (the White Rose) is possibly the most spectacular moment of resistance that I can think of in the twentieth century.... The fact that five little kids in the mouth of the wolf, where it really counted, had the tremendous courage to do what they did, is spectacular to me. I know that the world is better for them having been there, but I do not know why." In the same issue of *Newsday*, historian Jud Newborn noted that "You cannot really measure the effect of this kind of resistance in whether or not X number of bridges were blown up or a regime fell ... The White Rose really has a more symbolic value, but that's a very important value."

On February 22, 2003, a bust of Sophie Scholl was placed by the government of Bavaria in the Walhalla Temple for prominent Germans located near Regensburg in Bavaria. The Scholl Siblings Institute for Political Science at Munich University is named for Sophie and Hans Scholl. Many local schools as well as countless streets and squares in Germany have been named after the Scholls. In 2003, in  a nationwide competition to choose the top ten most important Germans of all time, Sophie Scholl and her brother Hans finished in fourth place, above Bach, Goethe, Gutenberg, Bismarck, Willy Brandt and Albert Einstein. If the votes of young viewers alone had been counted, Sophie and Hans Scholl would have been ranked first. Earlier, readers of *Brigitte*, a German magazine for women, voted Sophie Scholl "the greatest woman of the twentieth century".

CINEMA, LITERATURE AND THEATER

In the 1970s and 1980s, there were three film accounts of Sophie: Scholl and the White Rose resistance. The first film entitled *Das Versprechen* (*The Promise*). was financed by the Bavarian state government and released in the 1970s. In 1982, Percy Adlon's *Five Last Days* presented Lena Stolze as Sophie Scholl in her last days from the point of view of her cellmate, Else Gebel. In the same year, Stolze repeated the role in Michael Verhoeven's *Die Weisse Rose*. In February 2005, the movie about Sophie Scholl's last days, *Sophie Scholl—Die letzten Tage* – (The Final Days), featuring actress Julia Jentsch in the title role, was released. It was nominated for an Academy Award for Best

Foreign Language Film in 2006. For her portrayal of Scholl, Jentsch won the best actress at the European Film Awards and the Silver Bear for best actress at the Berlin Film Festival.

In literature, *Shattering the German Night* (1986) about the White Rose by Jud Brown and Annette Dumbachs was reissued in an illustrated edition in 2006 as *Sophie Scholl and the White Rose*. In February 2009, History Press released *Sophie Scholl: The Real Story of the Woman Who Defied Hitler* by Frank McDonough. And in February 2010, Carl Hanser Verlag released *Sophie Scholl: A Biography* by Barbara Beuys in German. Playwright Lillian Garrett-Groag's play *The White Rose* features the person, Sophie Scholl. *We Will Not Be Silent*, a drama by David Meyers of Sophie Scholl's imprisonment and interrogation premiered at the Contemporary American Theater Festival in Shepherdstown, West Virginia in July 2017.

# Walter Benjamin on the Jewish Question
## And
## Theses on the Philosophy of History

On Reading Hannah Arendt's Introduction to Benjamin's
*Illuminations*


German-Jewish intellectuals, the alienated *hommes de lettres* of early twentieth century German-speaking Central Europe, constituted a class within that complex, multi-layered Jewish society against which a few of them rebelled, a rebellion which however could not prevent the dark disaster awaiting them in the German nightmare of the 1930s and 40s. Walter Benjamin (1892-1940) was one of those rebels.

Hannah Arendt's 51-page introduction to Benjamin's world is a powerfully interpretive book in itself, which by no means is separate from the book that she introduces and also edits: she is a necessary part of the author's *Illuminations* because in the story of an intellectual figure of the stature of Benjamin there are multiple variants and interpretations of his message. Hers is one of those. With one eye of Arendt, I have reported in these pages what I find stimulating and central to this man, who did not become widely known until some twenty years after his death in 1940 ... after which he became the cult figure he is today. The subjects Arendt deals with are humbling to the reader striving to grasp the historical moment of a century ago, a moment that she warns "was washed away, as it were, by the catastrophe of European Jewry and is justly (largely) forgotten." Nonetheless, the reader recognizes the immediacy of many of the issues raised in her work about Benjamin and their applicability today, if only to confirm his aversion to Zionism and/or the Jewish State of Israel. Such are the considerations that most German-Jewish intellectuals of the early 1900s faced, though indecisively, as Arendt, too, goes on to show.

Walter Benjamin was a German-Jewish thinker, one of a handful of *hommes de lettres* as Arendt defines him: people who lived in the world of books but were not obliged to write them for a living; thus they were alienated from both the state and the society of those times. He lived in Berlin and Paris, and ultimately killed himself in the mountains between France and Spain trying to escape the Nazis and get to America. You might also think of Benjamin in relation to chance because of his up and down relationship with both good and bad chance. Mostly the latter. And it was what killed him. Killed him because he was also a self-defined bungler. He lived in Germany but apparently seldom felt at home there; his most beloved place was Paris whose streets gave birth to the figure of Benjamin's *flaneur*, the stroller-idler-bohemian which became a key figure in his writings.

Although Benjamin called himself a literary critic, he was concerned with the truth content of a literary work and left its subject matter to the commentators. True to his nature, however, he was much more than a literary critic. He wrote studious works but was not a scholar. In a similar fashion, he was a Marxist but never joined the Communist Party, a non-decision that kept him free of that—for this writer—hateful anticommunist left. Those American Leninist anticommunist intellectuals in Greenwich Village of the late thirties-early forties, the "respectable left" that Saul Bellow writes of who considered the Russian revolution a failure and were content to think the right thing but do nothing for it, content to set positions for the others. For some twenty years Benjamin considered emigration to Palestine but never immigrated. He was not a translator but did magnificent translations into German of Baudelaire and Proust. He was not a poet but he wrote poetically. BUT, his being a bungler made him a pushover for the god Chance whose fickleness in his regard made him an even greater bungler. Calamities happened to him time and again. Arendt recalls that bad luck often visited him, bad luck personified in German fairytales as a little *hunchback*. Like when a publisher finally accepted one of his major books the publishing house promptly folded. The little hunchback had intervened. Again, Benjamin escaped Nazi Germany and settled in his beloved Paris. Then when the Nazis were about to bomb Paris he fled to Meaux, East of Paris—*toward* the Germans he was escaping from. For his safety, he thought. Then the Germans didn't bomb Paris after all but bombed Meaux, a troop center. *Pfusch*! Bungled again. The little hunchback had visited him again. His whole life went like that. Then he bungled right up to the end and he paid the god Bad Chance with his life. Benjamin had obtained an emergency U.S. visa from a consulate in unoccupied France, had a Spanish transit visa for Portugal and had secured ship passage to the USA. But he didn't have a French exit visa which the Vichy government refused him as a German Jew. This was not a great problem since you could easily walk over a mountain path from France to Port Bou in Spain and then travel on to Lisbon. But on that one day—not the day before or the day after—Spain rejected his transit visa. In desperation because of his heart condition, again bungling and with the god Bad Chance and the little hunchback against him, he decided to end it all then and there. He didn't take the rest of the walk.

Walter Benjamin's death prompted his friend, the poet Bertold Brecht, in exile in Denmark, to remark that this was the first real loss Hitler caused to German literature. Benjamin himself was certainly not oblivious to politics; he took it seriously, but, as his life showed, not seriously enough to protect himself from it. According to Chekhov, "A bit of ideology and being up to date is most apropos.

At the beginning of her introduction, Hannah Arendt notes that posthumous fame seems to be the lot of unclassifiable writers, which Benjamin clearly was. Never a writer who furnished avid readers with information, his imagination took flights simply incomprehensible to the reader in search of excitement or even explicit morality. Yet, since his life was cut short by Nazism, he never succumbed to the temptation to become a journalist. Nor did he even consider the idea of becoming a specialist; therefore, he remained the non-academic per se. Respectability as an end remained forever alien to Walter Benjamin. After reading his works you would also hesitate to classify Benjamin as an intellectual of the type Sartre or Régis Debray. Everything he wrote was sui generis, in the same way that Kafka was unique. Neither fit into the existing order, nor did they introduce a new genre for future writers. For example, Hugo von Hofmannsthal wrote that Benjamin's long essay on Goethe was literally "absolutely incomparable." It would be just as misleading to classify Benjamin as a literary critic—as he called himself—and essayist as to label Kafka simply a short-story writer and novelist. Benjamin's unclassifiable status must have contributed in a major way to his isolation and aloneness, within which he saw beauty and paradox, for him always phenomena ... both of which seemed fugitive and ungraspable.

## The Jewish Problem in the German-Speaking World

The Jewish problem was twofold according to Moritz Goldstein—Benjamin's life-long friend—in an article "German-Jewish Mt. Parnassus" published in 1912 in the prestigious journal, *Der Kunstwart*: on the one hand, the non-Jewish environment which hated and rejected Jews and, on the other, assimilated Jews who wanted to remain Jews but did not want to admit their Jewishness either. Goldstein believed the problem insoluble. Yet his aim was to force them to admit their Jewishness or be baptized, even though he and other Jewish intellectuals realized that would solve nothing. The case of Edith Stein was exemplary: born in a non-observant Jewish family in Breslau, studied at Freiburg and Göttingen universities, converted to Catholicism, philosopher, close to phenomenologist Edmund Husserl, she died anyway in a gas chamber in Auschwitz on August 9, 1942. Declared a martyr and saint, she became one of six co-patron saints of Europe.

No getting around it: German hate was genuine hate. Ineradicable. So "our relationship to Germany is one of unrequited love", Goldstein wrote, which we should "tear out of our hearts ... but cannot."

Like Benjamin, also Kafka fought against the attitude of official middle class Jewry with whom intellectuals like themselves hardly had contact: their lying denial of the very existence of widespread anti-Semitism. Benjamin called such writing "a major part of the vulgar anti-Semitic as well as of Zionist ideology." Arendt quotes Kafka on the same subject of the insolubility of the Jewish problem for German-Jewish writers like himself: "… they lived among three impossibilities: the impossibility of not writing; the impossibility of writing in German—Kafka considered their German language as stolen and someone else's possession"—and the impossibility of writing differently" since no other language was available. "And," he added as a fourth, "the impossibility of writing, for this despair could not be mitigated through writing."

Arendt notes that that it was hard to take these problems seriously since they could be misinterpreted as mere reaction to the anti-Semitic environment of that era. But not for intellectuals of the stature of Benjamin and Kafka who were not criticizing anti-Semitism as such. They criticized that Jewish middle class for their denial of the very existence of anti-Semitism, as well as their—middle class Jews—isolation deriving from their loss of reality which was backed up by the wealth of those same classes. And besides they also blamed the Jews from Eastern Europe, the *Ostjuden*, for any existing anti -Semitism. Benjamin and Kafka fought against the rich Jewish middle class because "it would not permit them to live the world as it happened to be, without illusions". Important was the reality that very few German-Jewish writers saw the problem as did Benjamin and Kafka because most of them belonged to that same middle class that they criticized. Kafka labeled such German-Jewish middle class writers "the hell of German-Jewish letters." They were truly living in an incubus.

Hannah Arendt: "For the Jews of that generation the available forms of rebellion were Zionism and Communism, and it is noteworthy that their fathers often condemned the Zionist rebellion more bitterly than the Communist. Both were escape routes from illusion into reality, from mendacity and self-deception to an honest existence. But this is only how it appears in retrospect," she notes. "At the time Benjamin tried a half-hearted Zionism and then a no less half-hearted Communism, the two ideologies faced each other with the greatest hostility: the Communists were defaming Zionists as Jewish Fascists and the Zionists were calling the young Jewish Communists 'red assimilationists'." Gruesome pogroms during the Russian Civil War resulted in waves of Jewish emigration to Israel and accelerated the acquisition of Palestinian lands by legal Jewish emigrants, the subject of a Spanish novel by Julia Navarro, *Dispara, yo ya estoy Muerto*, in English, *Shoot Me, I'm Already Dead*. In the novelist's presentation many of the early Jewish settlers who bought their lands near Jerusalem legally were Socialists/Communists and their small farms and orchards were organized as communist collectives. Today's Israel is another story: there are roughly only 270 kibbutzim left, with about two percent of the population.

For those German-Jewish rebels it was as if the solution to their problem was to be found in either Moscow or Jerusalem; however, Benjamin—like Kafka—knew all the time that his productive life was in Europe. At the same time, neither of them wanted to return to the ranks of the Jewish people or to Judaism, not because they were too "assimilated in the German language area and too alienated from their Jewish heritage, but because all traditions and cultures as well as all belonging had become equally questionable to them. And this was also why they couldn't return to the Jewish fold as proposed by the Zionists." (Arendt)

Still, that rare person that was Benjamin translated his personal conflicts into a more radical problem and questioned the Western tradition in toto. Therefore Marxism and the Communist revolutionary movement attracted him because it opposed the totality of political and spiritual traditions.

But the bulk of those European Jews of East and West followed the Zionist pied-pipers to Palestine, founded a state of their own on stolen property and became a quasi-European, right-wing state on land "stolen and someone else's possession"—as

Kafka had referred to the German Jews and the German language—and named it Israel, and the Jewish People, the Hebrew Nation. One is left to wonder if they had really resolved the insoluble Jewish problem of last century before the nightmare became tragedy: in any case, they retain their Jewish identity within their own nation-state, Israel, artificial as it may be on another people's land.

In a sense then Benjamin decided not to decide. However, his point of departure always seemed to be the utter destructive basis of Fascism. His search in Zionism—discarded before entering its labyrinth) and in Communism which he never adopted, perhaps because of the growing bureaucracy he saw in Communist Russia when he went to Moscow in 1926 and which might have reminded him of the official Jewry he was escaping from. His search for alternatives shines through in his memorable *Theses on the Philosophy of History*.

## "Theses on the Philosophy of History"

Walter Benjamin completed this remarkable eleven-page *writing* in the spring of 1940, the last year of his life. It was first published in *Neue Rundschau* in Berlin, a quarterly magazine founded in 1890 and which has existed well over one hundred years, publishing the best of European writing, essays and fiction, by authors such as Rainer Maria Rilke, Thomas Mann and Franz Kafka. Hannah Arendt writes that shortly before his death Benjamin gave her a copy of the manuscript which contains, however, many variants written in his difficult to decipher handwriting. Her version of his eighteen Roman numbered paragraphs is included in the book *Illuminations*.

Benjamin thinking is complex thinking. His work is not material for tea party reading. He loves allusions and even resorts to the supernatural. His hobby after that of book collector—he collected books not to be read but to be possessed—was to collect quotes; he aspired to construct a book made up of only quotes.

And he himself left many of his own quotes for posterity … and for writers after him.

In his Theses, Benjamin devotes major attention to the defects of social democracy, to historical materialism and to the "state of emergency", the latter which in his view is not the exception but the rule. For purposes of simplification I have extracted chiefly his views on the disaster of Social Democracy. Therefore, as he affirms in paragraph VIII, the necessity of attaining *"a conception of history that is in keeping with this insight. Then we shall clearly realize that it is our task to bring about a real state of emergency, and this will improve our position in the struggle against Fascism. One reason why Fascism has a chance is that in the name of progress its opponents treat it as a historical norm.*

In general I have selected quotes that literally jump off Benjamin's pages, quotes which I list under their respective number without an attempt at comment. To some they will perhaps read like a listing of quotes. However, I believe his real subject in these *Theses* was the failure of Germany's Social Democracy, which paved the way for German Nazism-Fascism. For me the *Theses* were far from impromptu or conceived in that last year; they sum up matters he was writing about already in Berlin in his twenties. They sum up his life. The Benjamin legacy.

IV

The class struggle, which is always present to a historian influenced by Marx, is a fight for the crude and material things without which no refined and spiritual things could exist…. They have retroactive force and will constantly call in question every victory, past and present, of the rulers.

VI

Historical materialism wishes to retain that image of the past which unexpectedly appears to man singled out by history at a moment of danger …. That of becoming a tool of the ruling classes.

VII

And all rulers are heirs of those who conquered before them. Hence, empathy with the victor invariably benefits the rulers. Historical materialists know what that means. Whoever has emerged victorious participates to this day in the triumphal procession in which the present rulers step over those who are lying prostrate.

X

At the moment when the politicians in whom the opponents of Fascism had placed their hopes are prostrate and confirm their defeat (Social Democrats) by betraying their own cause, these observations are intended to disentangle the political worldlings from the snares in which the traitors have entrapped them.

XI

The conformism which has been part and parcel of Social Democracy from the beginning attaches not only to its political tactics but to its economic views as well. It is one reason for its later breakdown. Nothing has corrupted the German working class so much as the notion that it was moving with the current….it was but a step to the illusion that the factory work which was supposed to tend toward technological progress constituted a political achievement….it (work, he means) already displays the technocratic features later encountered in Fascism…..

XII

Not man or men but the struggling, oppressed class itself is the depository of historical knowledge….This conviction … has always been objectionable to Social Democrats….

XIII

Social Democratic theory, and even more its practice, have been formed by a conception of progress which did not adhere to reality but made dogmatic claims…. first of all, the progress of mankind itself…. Secondly, it was something boundless, in keeping with the infinite perfectibility of mankind. Thirdly, progress was regarded as irresistible, something that automatically pursued a straight or spiral course....

XIV

History is the subject of a structure whose site is not homogeneous, empty time, but time filled by the presence of the now. (*Jetztzeit or* 'now time') Thus, to Robespierre ancient Rome was a past charged with the time of the now (time) which he blasted out of the continuum of history…. A tiger's leap into the past. This jump, however, takes place in an arena where the ruling class gives the commands….

XV

The awareness that they are about to make the continuum of history explode is characteristic of the revolutionary classes at the moment of their action. The great revolution introduced a new calendar. The initial day of a calendar … is the same day that keeps recurring in the guise of holidays, which are days of remembrance. Thus calendars do not measure time as clocks do; they are monuments of a historical consciousness. …

XVI

A historical materialist cannot do without the notion of a present which is not a transition, but in which time stands still…. Historicism gives the "eternal" image of the past; historical materialism supplies a unique experience with the past … man enough to blast open the continuum of history.

XVII

Historicism rightly culminates in universal history. Materialistic historiography differs from it as to method…. Universal history has no theoretical armature. Its method is additive; it musters a mass of data to fill the homogeneous, empty time. Materialistic historiography, on the other hand, is based on a constructive principle.

Here I have substituted Benjamin's XVIII with his number IX as a conclusion:

XVIII

A Klee painting named "Angelus Novus" shows an angel looking as though he is about to move away from something he is fixedly contemplating. His eyes are staring, his mouth is open, his wings spread. This is how one pictures the angel of history. His face is turned toward the past. Where we perceive a chain of events, he sees one single catastrophe which keeps piling wreckage upon wreckage and hurls it at his feet. The angel would like to stay, awaken the dead, and make whole what has been smashed. But a storm is blowing from Paradise; it has got caught in his wings with such violence that the angel can no longer close them. This storm irresistibly propels him into the future to which his back is turned, while the pile of debris before him grows skyward. The storm is what we call progress.

# BERTOLD BRECHT

The German poet-playwright Bertold Brecht put Marxist collectivism and dialectical materialism into his art as few other Western writers and thus belied any doubts about his ultimate objective: ed-u-ca-tion of the people. And he meant education in Socialism. The existence of thirty volumes of Brecht's works will bewilder the many people who limit his art to *The Threepenny Opera* and images of Satchmo singing *Mack the Knife.*

From the moment Brecht became a Marxist in his late twenties he applied dialectical materialism first to his theatrical work: his chief targets were European post-WWI culture and in particular the German bourgeoisie and its war, reflecting his generation's disillusionment with the civilization that had crashed in the Great War. And like the better part of his generation he aimed at the defeat of capitalism.

Bertold Brecht was born in Augsburg near Munich in1898 and died in East Berlin in 1956. He studied medicine at Munich University (1917-21). A revolutionary city at the time, Munich was part of Germany's November Communist Revolution (1918-19) and at the same time the birth place of the Nazi movement led by Hitler and his Brown Shirts while Brecht wrote his poetry and conceived his arts. At age twenty-four and living in Munich, Brecht changed Germany's literary complexion. The Berlin critic Herbert Ihering wrote in his review of Brecht's first produced play, *Drums in the Night* (*Trommeln in der Nacht*) that "he has given our time a new tone, a new melody, a new vision ... a language you can feel on your tongue, in your gums, your ear, your spinal column." That year of 1922 while Hitler was organizing his Nazi Party, Brecht won the prestigious Kleist Prize—Germany's most significant literary award—for his first three plays (*Baal, Drums in the Night,* and *In the Jungle*).

Though his collaboration with the progressive Viennese composer Kurt Weill was important in his creative life, his major work was not *The Three Penny Opera;* his chief contribution was his dramaturgy, poetry, theoretical works and his own theater ensemble influenced by Meyerhold and Piscator. However, keen to revolutionize the tired bourgeois opera tradition in 1927 Brecht and Weill produced *Mahagonny Songspiel*, an operetta based on Brecht's *Mahagonny* poems which Weill set to music. Radical theater, the story set in a boxing ring relates the greed in the godless pleasure seeking city of Mahagonny.

The editors of the *Encyclopaedia Britannica* write extensively about Brecht's creative work: "The essence of his theory of drama … is that a truly Marxian drama must avoid the Aristotelian premise that the audience should be made to believe that what they are witnessing is happening here and now. For he saw that if the audience really felt that the emotions of heroes of the past—Oedipus or Lear or Hamlet—could equally have been their own reactions, then the Marxist idea that human nature is not constant but the result of changing historical conditions would automatically be invalidated. Brecht argued that the theatre should not seek to make its audience identify with characters on the stage; it should rather follow the epic poet's art which is to make the audience realize that what it sees on the stage is merely an account of past events that it should watch with critical detachment. Hence, the "epic" (narrative, nondramatic) theatre is based on detachment, on the *Verfremdungseffekt* (alienation effect, or defamiliarization), achieved through devices that remind the spectator that he is being presented with a demonstration of human behavior in a scientific spirit rather than with an illusion of reality, in short, that the theatre is only theatre and not the world itself." Brecht could have written that readers of this account here should not be made to identify with the Brecht of the 1920s and 30s and his generation's disappointments. Yet today we can see him as an "epic hero". A hero who faced historical conditions much different from ours. For a different set of reasons we too will likely be depicted by later historians as a disillusioned generation, a generation searching for solutions to threats of nuclear war and the destruction of planet Earth. Brecht instead had to face Adolf Hitler's Nazism in all is manifestations.

However, we can appreciate Brecht for his accomplishments in his era as a result of his application of the dialectical process: the underlying evil of capitalism marked his times—with or without Adolf Hitler—as it does ours. Though there are similarities between the conditions facing the Brechtian generation and ours today, there are major differences of degree: his generation had witnessed the destruction of a civilization in the Great War but nonetheless searched optimistically for the regeneration of society; instead our generation tends to be a demoralized but also placid generation, facing an Armageddon we perceive but which many ignore. Still, after all, disasters remain disasters not matter what the media and the statesmen say.

Read Bertold Brecht and you perceive the energy and hope of his generation; we today instead see around us a hopeless and/or disinterested generation, the majority of which is largely ignorant of the reality of our situation: we face the super power USA led by Strangelove-like psychopaths and their "Take it all" and *"après moi le déluge"* philosophy. Brecht's generation faced traditional old regional power blocs; we face the rise of immense geopolitical blocs covering the globe, hostile one to the other.

Walter Benjamin noted that his friend Brecht considered the task of the epic theater less the development of actions than the representation of conditions. That is, Marxism in action. Brecht aimed at depriving the stage of sensations derived from the subject matter; he recommended dwelling on "historical incidents and purging them of the sensational". Brecht's theater was conceived to speak didactically to the masses. For that he wanted a relaxed and receptive audience who could better follow familiar and easy to receive and digest situations. The class struggle, always present in Marxist writing, "is a fight for the crude and materials things without which no refined and spiritual things could exist." (Walter Benjamin)

BERTOLD BRECHT IN THE USA

Brecht's epic theater didn't work in the capitalist USA where he spent six of his twelve exile years, from 1941-1947. He lived in Los Angeles and was frequently in New York. But neither Hollywood nor Broadway understood his genius, no more than did the House Un-American Activities Committee understand his political orientation. James K. Lyon wrote in BERTOLT BRECHT IN AMERICA (Princeton University Press) that Brecht *"after five years in the hated capitalist U.S. could write: "No wonder that something ignoble, loathsome, undignified attends all associations between people and has been transferred to all objects, dwellings, tools, even the landscape itself."* The Marxist Brecht continued to see the capitalist USA as he did in his play Mahagonny. And in true Brechtian style he had no intention of conforming to America but instead tried to confirm his earlier model of it. A key to Brecht's Marxism was his emphasis on the collective while downplaying the individual. His art emphasized the primacy of the Leninist Party and demanded the total self-effacement of the Party worker. Lenin's teaching contained the proper standard of conduct and Bolshevism a way of life. So it was no wonder that his experience in the USA was a disaster.

His association with a new, post-Expressionist movement in German arts, New Objectivity (*Neue Sachlichkeit)* prompted him to develop his *Man Equals Man* (*Mann ist Mann*) project, a kind of collective—varying groups of collaborators with whom he henceforth worked. Following the idea of the collective vs. the individual, two films, Eisenstein's *Battleship Potemkin* and Chaplin's *The Gold Rush*, introduced Brecht to dialectical materialism and prompted him to closer studies of Marxism and socialism. In 1964 he revealed in (BRECHT, pp 23-24): "When I read Marx's *Capital* I understood my own plays….Marx was the only spectator for my plays I'd ever come across:" Brecht praised Bolshevik collectivism for the replaceability of each member of the collective in his play *Man Equals Man.*

The collective adaptation of John Gray's *The Beggar's Opera* with lyrics by Brecht and music by Kurt Weill, *The Three Penny Opera* (*Die Dreigroschenoper*), was the big hit in 1920s

Berlin, influencing music worldwide. After World War II, Hildegard Knef sang *Mackie Messer.* Popular singers such as Frank Sinatra and Louis Armstrong made hit recordings of the song called in English, *Mack the Knife.* A famous line from the work underscored the hypocrisy of the Church and the establishment in the face of working-class hunger. *Erst kommt das Fressen, dann kommt die Moral.* First the grub, then morality.

MAHAGONNY- The Opera Hitler Hated

Bertold Brecht who visited the Soviet Union was partial to the Soviet form of Socialist Realism. Even if he earlier recommended familiar old historical themes for his epic theater, he did not mean that the "good old days" of bourgeois culture were good. "Better to start with bad new ones," he wrote, "rather than those good old ones." Brechtian theater as a rule was representative of his theory of using unusual and intriguing situations for holding the attention of his audiences and for educating them—as in *The Rise and Fall of the City of Mahagonny.*

*Der Aufstieg und Fall der Stadt Mahagonny* is considered the masterpiece of the Brecht/Weill semi-collective. Its premier in Leipzig in 1930 caused an uproar by Nazis in the audience, but its Berlin premier in Berlin in 1931 (on the eve of Hitler's assumption of full powers) was a triumph. The story of the operatic play is that three criminals create the city of Mahagonny. Drinking, gambling, prize-fights and such are the sole occupation of the inhabitants. Money rules. Mahagonny is threatened by a hurricane which after causing much distress bypasses the city. But after the hurricane nothing is forbidden anymore and scenes of debauchery occur. The opera ends with discontent destroying the city, which burns as the inhabitants march away. It has a very contemporary ring.

The following excerpts from the article "The Opera Hitler Hated" by right-wing Rupert Christiansen published on March 10, 2015 in the conservative London *Telegraph* bombed *Mahagonny* on the eve of its performance at Covent Garden.

*"Does it belong in an opera house? And if not, where should it go? These are the twinned questions confronted by anyone addressing Bertold Brecht and Kurt Weill's vituperative musical satire Rise and Fall of the City of Mahagonny.... The text is barbed, ironic and challenging, the score richly textured and glitteringly seductive. But the great majority of attempts to give it theatrical life have fallen flat – it has bombed at both ENO (English National Opera) and the Salzburg Festival ... Mahagonny's origins lie in a half-hour concert cantata Mahagonny Songspiel ("sung play"), in which Weill set a selection of Brecht's poems about Mahagonny, a fictitious city in North America presented as a modern Sodom and Gomorrah, destroyed by its worship of graft and fraud, whisky and dollars.... Weill was happy with the idea that Mahagonny should be classified as an opera ... He wanted success, in other words, while Brecht wanted revolution.*

*In Germany, Mahagonny caused an even bigger scandal as an opera than it had as a Songspiel, and the fact that Hitler's insurgent Brownshirts often disrupted performances chanting the hideous Nazi Horst Wessel anthem only added to its notoriety. The catchy Alabama Song (sung by Lotte Lenya) became a popular hit, but Brecht was probably right in thinking that his insistence that capitalism rots the soul and screws us all was being swamped by the éclat of mere showbiz...."*

Brecht was known to "eat little, drink little and fornicate a great deal". He was certainly loved by few but hated by many, including Thomas Mann a fellow exile in the Los Angeles paradise and W.H. Auden, Brecht's most illustrious collaborator and translator and who knew him well. As the English actress Elsa Lanchester and singer of bawdy songs observed: "He was anti-everything, so that the moment he became part of a country, he was anti-that country."

The anticommunist religious fanatic who recounts in his memoirs how the Lord guided his every step in life, James K. Lyon in his book, *Bertold Brecht In America,* writes that people who knew him in America found him at least one of the following: rude, arrogant, dictatorial, opinionated, selfish and self-centered to the point of egomania, exploitative, unfeeling, lascivious, male-chauvinistic, parsimonious, shrewd, duplicitous, envious and mean-spirited. Professor Lyon explains his stance as a means to keep alive his indignation about social injustice. Brecht did drink sparingly, nothing stronger than an occasional glass of beer. Hence one of the most human moments in Lyon's book comes when a depressed Brecht, reeling from the unpleasantries and professional disappointments of his first encounter with New York and America back in 1935, resorted to carrying a flask of whiskey at all times. "I can't stand it here without whiskey," he complained to his fellow exile Hans Eisler.

Lyon also charges—naively even for him—that Brecht never criticized East Germany where he finally settled—retaining however his Austrian citizenship—and that he did not support the workers' uprising in East Germany in 1956. Of course Brecht didn't support an anticommunist uprising that smelled of CIA from the first moment. Those were Cold War times, things were never what they seemed in a period of the let's pretend way of life of intelligence warriors. Secret agents looked for other secret agents to send east or west. Like the East German STASI had its agents in the West, the CIA-controlled Nazi-infested Gehlen Org sent its agents to the East to spy and to stir up trouble: red-flag operations were the rule, regime change the goal. Brecht had to suspect the workers' uprising was a CIA false flag operation, as it surely was. Brecht did not join in the hue and cry of the anti-Stalinists either. (He won a Stalin prize.) Leninism was his standard of conduct and Bolshevism a way of life yet those standards never limited his spontaneity and inventiveness making him incapabable of absorbing new experiences

Still, whatever his personality and his Marxism-Bolshevism, Brecht was a genius and a great epic artist who like Saul Bellow back in the USA considered the Russian Revolution …"oh, so glorious." His many critics like Lyon were only critics, but he was Brecht.

## Field-Marshal Friedrich Paulus
## and
## Defeat at Stalingrad

I have long wondered if German Field-Marshal Friedrich Paulus really changed his loyalties after his defeat and his surrender of himself and the remnants of his famed Sixth German Army to the Soviet Red Army at Stalingrad in February 1943. Did he truly change his world outlook when as a prisoner of war in Soviet Russia he joined the National Committee for a Free Germany and the Anti-Fascist Union of German Officers? In order to save his life did he betray his entire background, his military career, his homeland that he had fought for and his Führer whom he had blindly followed? Was he a traitor to his beloved wife and to himself? Was his seeming change of heart genuine? When he broadcast anti-fascist messages to Germany over Radio Moskau were his words honest and sincere? Of course it is possible that on the road to Moscow after his surrender the Field-Marshal experienced a sudden illumination and like Saul, the persecutor of Christians on the road to Damascus, he too fell to the ground, underwent a metamorphosis from a killer of Soviet peoples in the hire of the Nazis and stood up transformed on the spot into an avid apostle for Socialist justice.

Thinking of the quandary of General Friedrich Paulus, complex questions surge spontaneously, questions to which Paulus himself would likely be unable to answer satisfactorily. Actually, the moral question for Paulus in itself would hardly merit such speculation were it not so rare a conversion at his level and in his place and time. In fact German Field-Marshals never knew defeat; and he was expected to kill himself first. But Paulus did not. Did he reject suicide only out of fear of death? That question too is germane, for from that first refusal followed the thirteen years of the rest of his debased and lonely life.

Therefore, since the acts of Field-Marshal Paulus of the German Wehrmacht affected not only himself but also the 300,000 men under his command—of whom only a handful survived—and since it also affected his homeland and his relationship to it, his wife and children, the life of Friedrich Paulus—as gray as it became—assumes extraordinary human significance. Many of us face life-changing situations which require risky if not daring decisions by ourselves—decisions concerning our whole way of life, in some cases concerning also our relationship with our homeland—but seldom do we face choices of the severity of that of Friedrich Paulus. For it is true that though people and times do change, certain characteristics, backgrounds and links will not let us go free ... as a rule the past is tenacious and unyielding. I personally think Paulus must have considered himself simultaneously both sincere and traitorous. Nonetheless, although betrayal can be sincere and sincerity can be traitorous, such decisions belong to the category of the bewildering and enormous acts which ancient Greek philosophers classified as decisions to be made by the gods ... and not by fearful mortal men.

Why write today about a German General at Stalingrad, seventy-five years since that epic World War II battle? The answer is that since most historians agree that Stalingrad was the turning point in World War II, making the failure of the German invasion of Russia ineluctable and as a consequence the collapse of Nazi Germany, Hitler's Thousand-year Reich, inevitable; it fits neatly into this look at the history of the some sixty years with which I am dealing in this book. There is however another aspect: since Paulus's Stalingrad is a momentous moment in that one key person's life—there is a similarity between Paulus's quandary lying on his bed under the ruins of Stalingrad to that of Napoleon in the moment of the reality of his defeat at Waterloo and in his exile sitting on the waterfront in Portoferraio on the island of Elba. Both must have seen their lives of victory pass before them time and again. A loyal man, Friedrich Paulus too, lying on his cot in his cellar headquarters under destroyed Stalingrad reviewed his life and took the momentous decision to betray his Führer, Adolf Hitler. For that reason I have attempted to get into his mind in order to grasp the essence of his thoughts as he arrived at the fateful decision to crossover to the side of the Soviet Union.

In June 1941, Nazi Germany undertook Operation Barbarossa in an atmosphere of fanfare and optimism. German blitzkrieg had already conquered most of West Europe. The German military machine—to a great extent financed by investors of the USA, France and Great Britain—seemed invincible; and now its blitzkrieg was loosed on Germany's tenuous partner in the division of Poland, its great enemy in the East, the Soviet Union, the USSR. First Germany's mighty artillery pounded Russian targets, then the Luftwaffe's Stukas and Messerschmitt's and Henkels zoomed eastwards with their loads of bombs made in Germany and the ferocious Tiger tanks made in Czechoslovakia crushed everything on their path between Poland and the heart of Soviet Russia, the Wehrmacht's unstoppable infantry mopped up, while the SS men brutally shot and hanged the Slav *Untermenschen* left behind. "We will be in Moscow by Christmas", Paulus's Führer gloated in the vein of Napoleon who supposedly said at Waterloo: "victory will be ours before the lunch hour."

But then the Germans encountered the lethal Russian winter . And what a winter. It overcame everything. Soundless and incomprehensible, an interminable deathly cold without interruptions, its slow steady insistence absorbed man, beast and machinery. German supply lines were interrupted. Blitzkrieg stalled at the gates of Moscow and Leningrad. Russia was not a cakewalk after all. No Christmas in Moscow; no New Year's in Leningrad. Yet General Paulus and his panzer divisions continued to race toward the oil fields in the Caucasus. Thousands of Germany's best young men were losing their lives but Paulus's panzer divisions plunged ahead undeterred on their useless flight eastwards while the General dreamed of the final victory to be achieved quickly once Russia's oil supplies were cut off.

Then—as if destiny had wormed is way into the scenario—Hitler saw Stalingrad on his maps. Stalingrad, right on Russia's supply routes. There stood the great city on the Volga, the city named for his enemy-in-chief. In his madness, Hitler had to have that city first of all ... and military strategy be damned. Thus because of a name on a map, Hitler lost his bet, Paulus lost his army, and Stalingrad was lost to the Russians who won World War Two on the River Volga. In Stalingrad. After that epic battle Russians could laugh at the puny Anglo Normandy invasion ... two years late and carried out chiefly so the Allies could share in the booty  and occupy the country that was Germany. The Red Army defeated Paulus's Sixth Army, then raced on westwards to win the war, and change the flow of history for which the USA has never forgiven Russia ... Russia's victory was not in the scenario.

But my questions about this one human being remain: Did Field-Marshal Paulus undergo an epiphanic transformation after he lost the battle of Stalingrad? Did the meticulous man who commanded the 300,000 soldiers of Hitler's famed Sixth Army really cross over to the victorious enemy? Did the man who loved family, Germany and Beethoven betray his Fatherland? Or, was Field-Marshal Friedrich Paulus—who sent tens of thousands of men to their deaths in the Stalingrad debacle—after all a coward? Hitler named General Friedrich Paulus Field-Marshal in the last hours of the catastrophe, not as a reward but as an invitation to suicide: no German Field-Marshal in history had ever fallen live into enemy hands. But Paulus did not die in Stalingrad.

Since reading the section about Paulus and Stalingrad, "The Last Field-Marshal", of William T. Vollmann's epic *Europe Central,* (page 328-410 in the Penguin edition), I have been asking myself that question: Did Paulus really change? Or did he live the rest of his life in a lie just to prolong his existence— apparently miserable. If not, what then are the real reasons for his betrayal? After a life of obedience to Prussian militarism first, and then to Adolf Hitler, did he truly become anti-Nazi and anti-war after his capture by Russian troops?

I repeat: the question is not rhetorical. Friedrich Paulus faced a dilemma much greater than ordinary people ever have to face in life. He was a military man. A Prussian soldier. Before and during the battle of Stalingrad he was faithful to "his" Führer. To his people. To his beloved wife to whom he wrote daily letters of love and devotion; and yet whom he also betrayed: she spent years in the Dachau concentration camp for his defection to the Communist Slavs.

I have read that the man, Friedrich Paulus, was reserved and uncertain of himself. But I find it difficult to believe he was truly a coward, too, although his external life did change dramatically soon after his capture by Russian troops. Was it then normal human fear that changed the man who commanded hundreds of thousands of soldiers and whose decisions conditioned the outcome of World War Two?

Declassified STASI (East German Intelligence) documents describe Friedrich Paulus as an energetic and ambitious man born in 1890 in the village of Guxhagen in the German state of Hessen, the son of an accountant. After brief studies at famous Marburg University, at the age of nineteen he enrolled in the army, the *Deutsches Heer* of the former German Empire, and fought WWI in offices and planning sections. He remained in the *Reichswehr* of the Weimar Republic, rising steadily through the ranks, a cold military professional who never joined the Nazi Party. In the Weimar period he trained Russian officers in Germany at which time he met the future Russian General Tukhachevsky who, according to STASI, once told Stalin presciently: "When Paulus is no longer needed in Germany, we can use him." Meanwhile Paulus married the daughter of Romanian aristocrats and had three children. When the Nazis arrived in power in 1933, Paulus, the professional soldier, "courageous and calm", became one of the non-political generals. Although in the Nazi era he became a General, he was allegedly reluctant to make great decisions without the approval of his Führer, to whom he seemed totally dedicated, an indication that he did not consider himself part of the ruling class for which Hitler—also an outsider—was an ignoramus to be replaced at the propitious moment

And so it was at Stalingrad. When he was finally encircled by Russian armies and his own generals urged an organized breakout of the encirclement, he tried to follow Hitler's orders: Fight to the last man. He vetoed the breakout proposal, but he did not fight to the last man. Lying in his cot in his headquarters in the cellars of Stalingrad's huge Universal department store he declared himself a "private person" and thus not a prisoner of war. He and his generals were taken to Moscow for interrogation and on August 8, 1943, six months after Stalingrad, he broadcast over Radio Moscow an appeal to German people charging his beloved Führer with the terrible war. He also testified in the Nuremberg trials against German Generals Jodl and Keitel. In Moscow he was rewarded: he lived in a luxurious dacha with servants.

I read German sources and the archives of STASI, State Security or *Staatssicherheit,* about Field-Marshal Friedrich Paulus. And I continued pondering the act of crossover from one ideology to another. Crossover for him meant changing from everything he had yet experienced in his military and family life to a new morality to the point of his own metamorphosis. Crossover points unwaveringly at transformation which is more than mere change; it is a different matter altogether. Most certainly he felt the kind of fear people feel at crucial turning points: he was making the decision to betray his beloved homeland, Führer, family and former life. Though any great change makes us anxious; even the change from a familiar place to another may make us feel uneasy. Concerning that familiar kind of change that we experience often, we are comforted by our awareness of being able to return to our original state. However, it is a different matter altogether when we lose our point of reference, our very sense of belonging, as Paulus had. "Calm and courageous" neo-Feld-Marshal Friedrich Paulus must have been panic-stricken when he became aware of the profundity and the darkness of the loss of his previous life gaping before him. He was going beyond, far beyond, what seemed human limits. He must have experienced that sensation of loss that triggers our deepest nostalgias and becomes a black hole in our existence, never to leave us for the rest of our life. On the other hand, perhaps a small part of Friedrich himself—tiny, minute, more an embryo of an idea of a new person deep inside his thus far isolated and alienated soul, a liberated Friedrich literally throbbing to live real life and sensing the occasion to become acquainted with personal freedom—was at the same time also transforming into a new being. There on his sagging cot, he may have felt new, unfamiliar impulses throbbing to express themselves, free of his familiar sense of loyalty and subservience and concomitant loneliness and anxieties. That is possible in a life.

Yet in any case, although I sympathize with Friedrich Paulus the man, I still have not decided what I believe moved the Field-Marshal to take the final step and defect to the side of Hitler's archenemy.

His crossover act was on another level, much more difficult than the proposed breakout from Russian encirclement which Field-Marshal Paulus vetoed. In the final analysis, I do not *believe* he truly made the crossover any more than he risked the breakout from the Stalingrad encirclement in disobedience of his Führer's orders to fight to the last man. Neither did he commit suicide as Hitler expected of him, nor did he and his soldiers fight to the last man as Hitler ordered; they went into captivity.

Perhaps Field-Marshal Paulus in the end decided not to decide. But not out of cowardice, I don't believe. We know the human mind is complex; the real reasons for one or the other of our great acts are usually unfathomable. And Paulus' times were difficult times; the decisions to be made were of a greater magnitude than those most of us mortals face in a lifetime. Although many of us have faced situations which posed great dangers to us—even to our way of life, in some cases also to our relationship with our homeland—the situation is seldom of the severity of that of Paulus.

Once a decisive man, he lost the capacity of rational purposefulness in his life choices in that time and place: his historical situation was greater than he was. So were his words sincere when he broadcast anti-fascist messages to Germany over Radio Moskau? Did Paulus betray his homeland that he had fought for, his wife and his beloved Führer in order to save his life? Was he a traitor to Germany, to everyone and to himself? Alas, times change but certain values remain intact. As above, I believe he was he was both. Both sincere and traitorous.

But my question about this one individual human being remains: Did Field-Marshal Paulus undergo an epiphanic transformation after he lost the battle? Did he truly cross over to the victorious enemy? Did the meticulous man change? Did the man who commanded the 300,000 soldiers of Hitler's famed Sixth Army of whom only 5000 returned to Germany after World War II change? Or, was Field-Marshal Friedrich Paulus—after sending tens and hundreds of thousands of men to their deaths in the Stalingrad debacle—after all simply a coward?

Such was the reality at Stalingrad: German defeat, Russian victory. When the Sixth Army was encircled by Russian armies and Paulus's own generals urged an organized breakout, his first reaction to their suggestion of disobedience was to follow Hitler's orders: he vetoed the breakout proposal. Wrapped as he was in a web of certainty that his army could not defeat the attacking Red Army, nor would it mutiny and attempt the breakout against his orders, he had to have perceived the weight of the stuff nightmares are woven of hanging over him. This timid man whose very life had been conformism and had always obeyed orders lacked the instinct to send the rest of his men to their certain death in the ruins of Stalingrad; everything had its limits, he discovered: even Hitler's orders had limits as did his loyalty to the Führer. He must have had horrendous visions of his army decimated to the last man in a Teutonic end times Armageddon. He strove to flee from such terror that he himself was obliged to order. Though not a fatalist, this man of reason and intellect who wrote daily letters to his Romanian aristocratic wife may have cursed a blind fate which refused to acknowledge his lifelong obedience. On the other hand, lying in his cot in his headquarters in the cellars of

Stalingrad's Univermag department store he had memories to deal with, memories of the happy dream world, of the good old times that he so wanted to experience again. Light had once shone on him and his family in the Fatherland and in a momentary intoxication from the bounteous happiness he perhaps imagined himself together again with his wife and children in a bucolic ambience where they would be *glücklich* forever. But that light quickly faded and extinguished and sadness and despondency filled his heart because he knew then it would not illuminate them again. Maybe then, still farther back in his mind, the University of Marburg passed before his eyes, a place he had loved but which like a faint streak of blue against the darkness of his recurrent thoughts it flashed past and was gone. He had to have known the terminology of the debates sweeping across the Europe of his period about Sigmund Freud's *unconscious mind*. He who had led the life of the conformist may truly have perceived ever so briefly the liberating suggestion of disobedience and insubordination rising from the depths of his unconscious.  After a life of obedience, after all the years of doing what was asked of him by his Leader, after following the rules and sending his men in their tanks to die on the road to the Baku oil fields and sacrificing tens and tens of thousands of young German men, the sudden urge to disobey and do the right thing overcame him. The great refusal blasted from him like the explosion of a Tiger tank when hit by Russian artillery, a repudiation of his own past and everything he had loved. He must have perceived the sudden sensation of freedom like a breath of fresh air. Though he had to realize that the feeling would be brief, the immediate sensation must have been glorious: the declaration of his personal freedom of the conformist, Friedrich Paulus.

Field-Marshal Paulus's visions of once-upon-a-time were relegated to obscurity and he took a non-decision and declared himself a "private person" … and thus not a prisoner of war. He appeared in the Nuremberg trials as a witness, not a defendant: he testified against other Germans.

After Stalin's death in 1953, Friedrich Paulus was allowed to settle in Dresden in the East German Democratic Republic, also there in a villa but under twenty-four hour STASI control. He met military officers of East and West and was active in a movement against West German rearmament and the Nazi-riddled Federal Republic of Germany in the West. He died in 1957 of ALS (Amyotrophic Lateral Sclerosis) in Dresden.

Crossover is no less difficult than the potential breakout from Russian encirclement at Stalingrad about which  Field-Marshal Paulus could not decide to do. So no, after that brief moment of freedom, I don't *believe* that Friedrich Paulus, in his heart, truly crossed over any more than he risked the breakout in disobedience of his Führer's orders. That too would have been beyond the limits. On the other hand he did not commit suicide as Hitler ordered and neither he nor his soldiers fought to the last man. Perhaps Field-Marshal Paulus decided not to decide the final issue either. But no, not out of cowardice. One false decision led ineluctably to another, and another, in a descending succession. In the magnitude of his time and place he lost the capacity to recognize limits and say a definitive "no". Field-Marshal Friedrich Paulus's historical situation was greater than was he the man.

# GLADIO

## THE STORY OF A CONSPIRACY

Albert Camus in his essay "L'Exil d'Hélène" discusses contemporary disregard for the Greek value of limits. Camus writes that only the artist by his nature recognizes his limits, limits which the historic spirit disregards. The very idea of a super-secret organization like Gladio to remake the world in its own image reflects that same disregard for the Greek values that Camus so cherished.

When in the early 1970s an Italian right-wing journalist told me about a secret army training in Italy's mountains, I scoffed at first thinking he was repeating a rumor picked up from some scoop-obsessed reporter. But my tune began changing when he gave it a name—"Stay Behind Army"—and explained it was a secret army to fight the Soviet armies which someday soon would invade West Europe. He gave me the name of a member of that secret army who would talk with me.

A few days later on a street corner near Rome's Sapienza University I met a sleazy-looking Roman in his early twenties accompanied by a no less unattractive friend. While we spoke both of them kept looking around us as if checking for tails. Their behavior was that of men on the run, yet who believed they were also men of destiny. They talked readily and I—without realizing it—was being shown a speck of a new planet. Speaking softly in a crisp language with their Rome accents, they said they had just finished a military training course in the nearby Abruzzi Mountains after having done basic training in Sardinia. Several times they used the term "Secret Army", lowering their voices and glancing around each time they pronounced the words. And no, they answered, the organizers would not allow journalist visits, and that yes, the secret army was well equipped and ready.

Years later, in the late 1980s or early 90s, it happened by chance that I met in a Rome hotel bar an American who knew details about that secret army. I was sitting on a stool at the bar of the luxurious Grand Hotel waiting for an appointment with a well-known writer when the man sat down on the stool next to me. I soon recognized William Colby from pictures of him in the press announcing the presence in Rome for a conference of the former Director of the CIA. I nodded, said hello, and we chatted bar talk until the chat turned into a short interview, which I subsequently published in the European press. I told him I knew who he was, and as we spoke I asked him point-blank about the mysterious Stay-Behind Army.

To my enormous surprise Colby almost boasted that the covert action branch of the CIA to which he was attached in the 1950s built throughout Western Europe what in intelligence trade parlance were known as 'Stay-Behind Nets', in Italy known as Gladio, the headquarters of which was in Rome. In that post-war period Colby was a young intelligence officer assigned to the CIA station in the US Rome Embassy. Officially the network was clandestine, he related, ready to be called into action as sabotage forces when the time came, thus confirming the few words of those two young Romans of years earlier. Colby said that in 1951 the chief of the CIA in West Europe sent him to the field to help build the Stay-Behind network. 'Our aim was the creation of an Italian nationalism capable of halting the slide to the left,' he said, as if speaking of ancient Greek history.

Officially, Operation Gladio—the code name of the clandestine Stay-Behind Net—was founded on November 26, 1956, to defend Europe from invasion by Warsaw Pact nations. Gladio was a CIA-Italian operation from the start and linked to NATO. However, it belonged heart and soul to the CIA. Gladio was officially dissolved on July 27, 1990. Or, as is likely, the operation assumed another name. Al Qaeda has been named as its successor.

After World War Two many top US military personnel had favored marching straight on to Moscow: Russia was their real enemy. Allied armed forces were then still fresh while Western Intelligence knew of the enormous Soviet war losses and that the mood of the Russians was to return home. Moreover many coopted German military and intelligence leaders repeated over and again: 'The time is now. Together we can crush Communist Russia.' Yet Allied leaders also knew well of the historical capacity of Russians to resist. No one could forget the disasters of Napoleon and Hitler in Russia. Saner appraisals favored prudence. The long Cold War was the result.

Although it existed and was fought, for more discerning minds knew the Cold War was a sham. A cover. If the Cold War was a certain guarantee of relative peace, the One World Order without limits was already burgeoning in the minds of secret powers in the western world. And Gladio was one of its newer weapons.

An *occupied country* atmosphere haunted Europe, especially Italy and Germany. US troops were everywhere and showed no signs of going back home. At the same time, unbeknownst to the troops and to Americans at home, the Gladio-Stay-Behind complex was growing. It had settled in for the long haul. Though Soviet tanks never arrived, Gladio helped keep occupied Europe in line. Terrorism was the means. Social unrest, changing borders and ethnic protests required attention. Then the rise of Socialist parties had opened a new front: Gladio had to tame overly ambitious socialists like François Mitterrand, Willy Brandt and Olof Palme. Sweden's Social Democratic Prime Minister, Palme, opposed the Vietnam War and maintained good relations with Castro's Cuba, with Allende in Chile and the Communist bloc of nations. In 1986, Olof Palme was assassinated on the streets of Stockholm. His killer was never found but it is reasonable to suspect a Gladio connection.

In the late 1950s terrorism erupted in north Italy when the separatist *Committee For the Liberation of the South Tyrol*, or BAS from the German *Befreiungsausschuss Südtirol,* spread terror in the Italian Tyrol. Already then in that early post-war terrorists were manipulated by the CIA as it did in Italy's northern region. Tyrolean people loved the terror they believed was perpetrated in the name of their secession from Italy and union with Austria—357 attacks causing the death of twenty-one people in thirty-two years of terror. But people did not know that BAS had become a CIA operation and in effect ran *against* their desire for secession. At first it had all seemed so easy to Tyroleans. A Rasputin-like priest, Michael Gamper, and nine militant activists founded BAS. Their goal: secession of South Tyrol from Italy and unification with Austria of the entire Tyrol, north and south. The CIA did not share that goal. In CIA minds Tyrolean unification with Austria with its strong Communist Party (KPO) was a nightmare: it would open a corridor from Soviet-occupied Eastern Austria for Soviet tanks headed for Rome. As BAS distributed pamphlets and destroyed symbolic places, the CIA and NATO saw the mouth-watering opportunity BAS terrorism offered. BAS terrorists were international with close ties to neo-Nazi organizations in Austria and Germany, they too infiltrated and used by the CIA. On *Fire Night* in June of 1961, BAS commandos destroyed thirty-seven electrical towers, interrupting the power supply of all of Upper Italy. That violence prompted a ready and willing NATO (now including the newly created secret army of Gladio) and Rome to intervene and crush the secessionist movement. Carrot and stick rule over mutinous Tyrolean-Italians. And according to the script US/NATO power had set things right: an early example of the *strategy of tension* at work. First, create the terror. Then, suppress the popular secessionist movement. There would be no secession here. Clearly the South Tyrol would remain Italian Alto Adige. It would not unite with North Tyrol. It would not become part of dangerous Austria. A whole panoply of evidence confirms the Tyrol-as-laboratory to test the CIA *strategy of tension*. And the groundwork was laid so that it was no surprise that a decade later, Italy's Marxist-Leninist Red Brigades imitated BAS tactics; in the end both Tyrolean terrorists and the Red Brigades were manipulated by Gladio. They were the actors in the *strategy of tension*. And now Gladio-Italy itself made a model: if the secret army conspiracy functioned so well in Italy, it would work in other European countries.

North Italy also made a model for Flemish terrorists in those late Fifties and the Sixties in Belgium when Brussels was considered a most dangerous city. And again during Belgium's "Bloody Eighties" and the Flemish rebellion against the French-speaking Wallon urge for power. Belgium's own secret army worked as efficiently as in Italy.

*Tension strategy* exists for the manipulation and control of public opinion: fear, propaganda, disinformation, psychological warfare, agents provocateurs … and false flag terrorist actions. Gladio's raison d'etre in Italy: organize terrorism and blame it on Communists; spread fear and then pass laws restricting the freedoms of the people. As they had done in the Alto Adige when people fell for the propaganda of the threat of a Soviet invasion and the scary image of Russian Cossacks watering their horses in Vatican fountains. But people just never decipher the simple formula. They are too afraid to face such obvious realities. More special laws are passed and thousands of leftists are imprisoned. Keep the populace afraid so that promises of security will be believed. You create fear with lies. The state media define Communists as the enemy and the state then suppresses dissent. Anything is justified to crush them. Communism and terrorists and Islamic fundamentalists … and today 'immigrants'. Gladio made a major contribution to the creation of an obedient Europe. Obedience however should be at the rupture point because the USA has exceeded all limits; but that is not the case. As if fearful of a world without US domination, Europe continues to fall in line.

People in Italy, in Europe—in the western world—know nothing about Gladio and the *strategy of tension*. They do not know why terrorism persists … nor who the real terrorists are. Today, in July, 2021, warnings sound from the government of the U.S. vassal state of Italy of ISIS threats against Italy specifically. ISIS or the Islamic State of Iraq and Syria, is an internationally active U.S. supported/financed and often sponsored Middle Eastern terrorist organization that moves its troops seemingly at will across the Middle Eastern and North African world. ISIS and

Gladio live in the same world creating a chaotic wasteland wherever its brand new trucks travel.

Italy's parliamentary investigations of Gladio resulted in a 300-page report on Gladio operations in Italy and its connections with the United States. Yet people are ignorant of that report that explains Gladio and casts the blame on the USA for the terrorism in Italy in the *years of lead* in the 1970s and 80s. It shows that the massacres, the bombings and paramilitary actions were organized by shadowy men within Italian state institutions—by men linked to American Intelligence. A bomb inside the Banca Nazionale dell' Agricoltura on Milan's Piazza Fontana on December 12, 1969 marked the continuation of the *strategy of tension: the Piazza Fontana massacre*. Sixteen dead, fifty-eight injured. The bombing took place at the height of the biggest strike wave that Italy had seen since the end of WWII. In those times automobile and sheet metal workers were militant and aggressive in those times. Trade unions dominated headlines. The word *agitation* was in wide use. Governments rose and fell as strikes and demonstrations became daily. Inflation drove prices to the sky, soaring interest rates, tottering governments, power outages and water rationing, second, third and fourth houses for the new rich and evictions for the poor. The people were incensed ... until the bombs on Milan's Piazza Fontana. Those bombs stopped the spread of agitation and the strike wave dead. The police hauled suspected leftist sympathizers in for questioning and intimidated their families while the government passed emergency laws against suspected terrorists. Hand in hand police and the media then blamed the Piazza Fontana bombing on a pathetic group of anarchists, the Bakunin Club, which anyway was already penetrated by the Italian secret services. An anarchist was pushed to his death from a fourth-story window of police headquarters in Milan.

More than twenty years after the bombing, official sources revealed that the bombs in the Piazza Fontana bank were placed by Gladio operating under the control of NATO intelligence worried that the strike wave would lead to the entry of the Italian Communist Party into the Rome government. Throughout the seventies and into the eighties NATO and Italian ruling circles were obsessed with keeping the Communists out of the government, culminating in the abduction and murder of Prime Minister Aldo Moro in 1978 for his attempts to bring the Italian Communist Party into the government coalition. The Moro murder was executed by the CIA/Gladio-run Red Brigades. The general public knew nothing about the real perpetrators: Gladio. They still do not.

A romantic time in Old Europe? Hardly. Soldiers in full battle dress patrolling the streets of Rome. Sirens screaming citywide day and night. Once in 1978 I returned from Iran with two of my Italian businessmen bosses and a very Eastern-looking Iranian customer. It was the day Premier Moro was abducted by the infiltrated and CIA-manipulated Red Brigades. While we drove around the city police stopped us five times for identification and searches. Two Italians, an American and an Iranian in the same car were suspect. Tension was rife in Rome. The abduction of the Premier exemplified the *strategy of tension* method of social control

It is a mystery that so few know anything about Operation Gladio. Despite the 300-page Italian parliamentary report, despite mentions even in the New York Times, despite coincidences like William Colby's free-and-easy revelations in a Rome bar, despite studies and articles about it in the leftist press, and despite decades of its nefarious activities worldwide which know no limits, people have remained ignorant about the US/NATO-run Operation Gladio.

## NAZISM IN THE DIASPORA
### Stepan Bandera—the Most Hated Man
### Who Ever Lived

There was no sun, no shadows. The star Wormwood had fallen from the heavens and polluted the earth's waters and after diminishing the shadows, had erased them. The falling of the stars had darkened the earth until all shadows vanished. And in the darkness the seventh seal of judgment loosed from the bottomless pit Abaddon the Destroyer together with the plague of Nazism that swooped down on earth to kill the third part of men and then to hover over the shadowless fields, writing its messages in the earth. (My adaptation of the revelations of the Seventh seal)

Adolf Hitler left a deadly legacy behind him; his was a lethal historical mission to decimate mankind, the evil legacy that Abaddon himself could have scripted. As history continues to show us over and over his suicide in the bunker in a Berlin overrun by Red Army soldiers was by no means the end of the Nazism that he constructed in his own image: he was the Destroyer, risen from the fire of the bottomless depths to destroy human kind. One of the most biting twists of history is that his Nazism—in power in Germany for only twelve years (1933-1945)—was to sweep like a biblical Revelation over the earth. We have seen that same Nazi-infected  continuity in post-war Germany and in the USA, in Operation Condor in Chile and Argentina which wiped out the best of the youth of both countries, and in Mexico under the "revolutionary" Fascist dictatorship. And today, again, in Ukraine we witness in action Nazism in its usual crude form. The diaspora of Nazism and Nazis and of the children they have spawned and continue to spawn generation after generation recalls the falling star of Wormwood still spreading darkness over the Earth. The very spirit of the Ukrainian Nazi killer of Jews, Stepan Bandera, assassinated in Munich in 1959, defines and infects the U.S.-constructed, assembled and managed Nazi-inspired government in Kiev Ukraine brought into being by the Maidan coup and the overthrow of the legally elected government of Ukraine. The Nazi spirit of Stepan Bandera, in the flesh a disgusting and hated man, thrives and continues spawning its own children.

Western journalists covering the Euromaidan riots and murders in Kiev in late February of 2014 encountered an historical image that few recognized. The black-and-white image of pasty-faced Stepan Bandera was plastered everywhere in the Ukraine capital— on barricades, over the entrance to Kiev's city hall, and on placards held by demonstrators calling for the overthrow of the Russian-friendly President, Viktor Yanukovych. So who in the hell *is* this Bandera, the journalists wondered.

People like Victoria "Fuck the EU" Nuland defined Bandera as a Ukrainian nationalist. The U.S. State Department spokeswoman accepted only praise and support for a Nazi regime in Kiev … come hell or high water and fuck European Union's objections an warnings not to disturb the Russian bear on its very border. When Russians charged he was a Nazi and an anti-Semite, Western media obediently labeled the truth as Moscow propaganda. Because of the official U.S. involvement foreign journalists quickly hedged in their reports from the Kiev Maidan. The *Washington Post* reported that Bandera had had only a "tactical relationship' with Nazi Germany and that his followers "were only *accused* of committing atrocities against Poles and Jews." For the *New York Times* Bandera had been slandered by Moscow as a pro-Nazi traitor. *Foreign Policy* dismissed Bandera as "Moscow's favorite bogeyman and metonym for all bad Ukrainian things." According to the best of the media, whoever Bandera was he couldn't have been as nasty as Putin claimed. "Maidan" is the square in Kiev where the U.S. coup gave birth to the Nazi-led Ukraine, of which Stefan Bandera was one of the most illustrious forefathers. *Maidan* is a proto-Indo-European word probably of Persian origin and used in Turkish, Pakistani, Indian languages for a large space, a meeting place, parade grounds. I first encountered the word in Tehran where on a famous Meydan the Shah's soldiers killed hundreds or thousands of protesters during the Iranian Islamic Revolution. Though not used in Russian, the word seeped into the Ukrainian language from Turkic languages.

Especially in Central Europe historical figures flash across the horizon and then quickly fade into the gossamer past and oblivion. But this man Bandera? Who was he? The name of Stepan Bandera (b.1909 in West Ukraine, d. Munich1959) is today the symbol of Ukrainian Nazism, the symbol of the ideology and practice of the big, new-old nation of Ukraine, vassal of the USA, and a former Republic of the Soviet Union. But in the Ukrainian capital of Kyiv—better known in Russian as Kiev—once one of Russia's major cities, the name Stepan Bandera lives again. To his memory are dedicated streets, squares and monuments in Nazi Ukraine, especially in his native West Ukraine. Today, Nazis of all nationalities pay homage to his memory. In 2010, the pro-West President Victor Yushchenko issued a decree naming Bandera "Hero of the Ukraine". That same year the then controversial decree was annulled by the newly elected President, the pro-Russian, Victor Yanukovich. Then again, in 2015, a year after the Maidan coup and the overthrow of the democratic government, a great majority of the new U.S. installed and supported Nazi government run by the sons of Bandera and their Svoboda and the Right Sektor parties voted unanimously to proclaim Bandera a national hero. Men of the infamous *Nachtigall* (Nightingale) battalion that fought side by side with the Nazi Wehrmacht exterminating Jews and Ukrainians alike and the persons of the apparatus of Ukrainian Nazism also became national heroes. Those heroes were in power. In those same days Nazi Ukraine invited members of the Association of Foreign Journalists in Rome of which I was a member to visit Bandera's native Lviv, an organized jaunt in an attempt to gain the support of the international press. One still wonders that the European Union and its media not only did not protest against the coup, against a Nazi-led government in the middle of Europe—the question that prompted the famous response of Victoria Nuland, the real organizer of the Maidan: "Fuck the EU"—but it instead reported on European Union discussions concerning EU membership for Nazi Ukraine. Bluntly, official America told official Europe to fuck off. America ordered Europe to fall in line and obey orders. So that again we see the ugliness, brutality and vulgarity of real history. The real history that is real people doing ugly or beautiful things that seldom reach the pages of written history.

But informed people know better. Informed people know who Stepan Bandera and his followers are. Those terrible Russians were of course right all the time. For the vast majority of Russians today the term *Banderovtsy* or Banderite is even worse than *Liberal* applied to that small minority in Russia who worship Western things, yearn for America, the European Union and NATO and detest Putin and Russian nationalists. Much, much worse than a so-called opposition leader Alex Navalny in Russia about whose pitiful existence many Russians are in fact unaware … but everybody knows what a Banderite is.

Already in his lifetime the little Bandera—he stood five feet and two inches—a Russian-hating, West Ukrainian Nazi—was detested literally by everybody: his political opponents within the Ukrainian independence movement hated him as did many of his own allies and followers; Jews and Russian-speaking ethnic Russians in Eastern Ukraine revile him as a fascist traitor to his country and a terrorist who collaborated with the Nazis and whose followers murdered thousands of Ukrainians; even his German Nazi masters considered him despicable because he betrayed and murdered his own people; the masses of displaced Ukrainians living in West Germany after World War II hated him for his crimes against other Ukrainians; elements of the post-war German government and many of Germany's American occupiers hated him... even those he served; Poles hated him for his crimes against the Polish people; Russians hated him in a special way because Bandera, in his German SS uniform, was responsible for the elimination of hundreds of thousands of Russians, soldiers, prisoners of war and civilians alike; today his figure is hated by all Russians because of everything he stood for; Ukrainian immigrants in Russia hate him and dislike being called Banderites because they are Ukrainian.

Yet nationalists in western Ukraine today revere him as a patriotic freedom-fighter, a martyr who led the struggle for independence from the Soviet Union: Bandera remains a hero in the eyes of the growing number of extreme rightists and Nazis in today's nationalist, jingoistic Ukraine, among Ukrainian nationalists abroad and right-wing extremists elsewhere. To the joy of re-flowering Nazi-Fascist organizations and parties across Europe, the Nazi- Banderite *Svoboda* (Freedom) and *Pravy Sektor* (Right Sector) parties run things in today's Ukraine. Bandera's image is honored on a postage stamp while his memory has assumed founder-of-Ukrainian-nationalism proportions. Moscow Avenue in the Ukraine capital of Kyiv was changed to Bandera Avenue. Still, on the other hand, articles galore have emerged in the international press of the life of an ugly and justifiably hated man, especially in Polish, German and English writings which can be seen on the Internet.

Bandera was the son of a nationalist-minded Greek Catholic priest in Western Ukraine, formally known as Eastern Galicia-Volhynia. Stepan grew up as a self-punishing fanatic who is said to have stuck pins under his fingernails to prepare himself for torture at the hands of enemies. And that as a university student in Lviv (Lvov), he whipped himself with a belt. "Admit, Stepan!" he would cry out. "No, I don't admit!" Yet, his followers found Bandera hypnotic: "You couldn't stop listening to him."

Stepan enlisted in the Organization of Ukrainian Nationalists (OUN) at age twenty where he steered an already violent faction into more extreme directions. In 1933, he organized an attack on the Soviet consul in Lviv, killing an office secretary. A year later, he directed the assassination of the Polish

Interior Minister. He ordered the execution of two alleged informers and was responsible for other deaths when the OUN took to robbing banks, post offices, police stations and private households in search of funds.

A study by the German writer Rossoliński-Liebe of what drove Bandera's violence takes us through the times and the politics that captured Bandera's imagination. Galicia—more or less Western Ukraine —had been part of Austro-Hungary prior to WWI. The Polish-controlled western half of Galicia was incorporated into the newly established Republic of Poland in 1918; the Ukrainian-dominated eastern portion (of West Ukraine) where Bandera was born was absorbed also by Poland in 1921 following the Polish–Soviet War and in that period enjoyed a brief period of independence. Bitter at being deprived of a state of their own, Ukrainian nationalists there refused to recognize the Polish takeover and in 1922 responded with arson attacks on thousands of Polish-owned farms. Warsaw resorted to mass arrests. By late 1938, some 30,000 Ukrainian-Poles languished in Polish jails. Polish politicians spoke of the "extermination" of the Ukrainians while a German journalist who traveled through eastern Galicia in early 1939 reported that local Ukrainians were calling for Hitler to intervene and impose a solution of his own on the Poles. The conflict in the Polish-Ukrainian borderlands of mixed peoples, languages and cultures exemplified the ethnic wars that erupted throughout Eastern Europe as the legions of Adolf Hitler and Nazism approached in WW Two.

Bandera meanwhile moved ever farther to the right, reading the works of militant nationalists who dreamed of a united Ukraine stretching "from the Carpathian Mountains to the Caucasus", a Ukraine free of Russians, Poles, Magyars, Romanians, and Jews. He studied the works of Dmytro Dontsov, the ultra-rightist spiritual father who translated Hitler's *Mein Kampf* and Mussolini's *La Dottrina Del Fascismo* and taught that ethics should be subordinate to the national struggle.

I have included a brief excursion into the lands of North Central Europe—Poland and Ukraine (including former

Galicia)—because precisely these lands were the *Lebensraum,* the Living Space, Hitler pinpointed for German expansion, the main reason for Germany's quiet and rapid rearmament. Lebensraum was one of the pillars  of Nazi Germany's foreign policy. One small problem was that like Palestine these lands were inhabited by other peoples. So according to Hitler's Aryan ideology the peoples of those lands had to be eliminated and peopled by German settlers. Here in a nutshell we have German Nazism in action: rearmament, anti-Semitism against the massive Jewry, the Ostjuden, and racism concerning the non-Aryan Slavic untermenschen. The Organization of Ukrainian Nationalists (OUN) was marked by extreme anti-Semitism, a message which far overshadowed the spread of socialist ideas spreading in these borderlands since the beginning of the twentieth century. Historically, however, anti-Jewish hatred had branded Ukrainian nationhood since the seventeenth century when Ukrainian peasants, maddened by the exactions of the Polish landlords and their putative Jewish estate managers, engaged in vicious pogroms. Nevertheless, while the influence of the OUN spread in Ukraine, Socialism was also taking firm hold. The gruesome pogroms during the Russian Civil War resulted in waves of Jewish emigration to Israel and accelerated the early acquisition of Palestinian lands by Jewish emigrants, the subject of a Spanish novel mentioned earlier, *Dispara, yo ya estoy Muerto* (Shoot, I'm Already Dead), by Julia Navarro. A curiosity in the novelist's presentation is that many of the early Jewish settlers who bought their lands near Jerusalem were Socialists/Communists and their small farms were organized as communist collectives.  Still, in Ukraine anti-Semitic passions intensified in 1926 when a Jewish anarchist named Sholom Schwartzbard assassinated the exiled right-wing extremist Ukrainian political leader, Symon Petliura, in Paris. Such events spurred on the Jewish flight from East Europe to Palestine in the years following the Balfour Declaration in 1917 pertaining to the British commitment to the creation of a state of Israel in Palestine.

## POLISH-UKRAINIAN-RUSSIAN RELATIONS

Exactly where Russia's real western border lies—or should lie—is one of the most contentious circumstances in Eastern Europe today. Some understanding of social-political currents in the huge area between Germany and Russia—that is, Poland and Ukraine—sheds light on the significance of the US fascist coup in Kiev of 2014 and the emergence of a fake country under US/NATO dominance. Ukraine with its 233,000 square miles is approximately the size of France with 248,000 square miles. The memory of the centuries-long confusion of past East Europe appeared like an open invitation to Hitler and Nazi Germany in its programmed quest for Lebensraum  and continues to influence EU/German policies today. So that the era beginning from World War II provides a useful starting point in understanding the current political role of Nazi Ukraine. Since Ukraine was part of the USSR, the Soviet Union's western border was its (i.e. the western border of the Ukrainian Socialist Republic) frontier with Poland. Today's Russia borders with a NATO-controlled and occupied Ukraine. Not the same thing at all.

Western Ukraine, particularly the city of Lviv-Lvov, occupies a special part of the Polish psyche—something like Kosovo for Serbs which NATO stole and where the USA built a huge military base, Camp Bondsteel. Therefore the separation of the former western portion of Ukraine, former Galicia, from the Polish state after WWII was hard for Poles to swallow despite the socialist ideology in East Europe at the time when nationalism was not supposed to take on emotional significance. Socialist solidarity between peoples counted more than nationalism; emphasis was on economic relations, not nationality. Nonetheless, the border changes proved to be a strategic miscalculation caused by blindness to the ever-present nationalism. At the time there was little that Poland could do about what it felt was the unfair dislocation of its eastern provinces with its many Ukrainians and peoples of complex and uncertain feelings of nationality.

Contemporary Poland has believed that the influence of the EU can re-establish its cultural and historical hegemony in its eastern regions. Poland believes it can rival Russia in terms of influence in those now western regions of Ukraine: whereas Russian influence is dominant in East Ukraine. Thus the German-dominated European Union, via Poland, has a strong influence in West Ukraine. On the other hand, the EU is also concerned about the quasi Fascist government of Poland: it worries that an unpredictable super-nationalistic Poland could consider a Polexit from the European Union, a defection that could topple an already shaky union. Moreover, such fears and hopes create confusion over both Polish and Ukrainian state identity.

Polish nationalists dream of their former great state. A kind of Polish Exceptionalism emerged from the influence of Polish Pope John Paul II (Karol Wojtyla) and Solidarity's historical victory over the communist government in 1989. Aided by God via the Polish Pope, Poles successfully defied Soviet power. Today Poles feel they have a future historical role because of their Exceptionalism. Poles believe their historical legacy entitles them to a major presence in Eastern Europe. And it wants its eastern lands back. Therefore Poland's particular opposition to Russia and *its* historical legacy. After the end of the Cold War, Poland decided on its pro-Western course of political and military development in order to pursue this destiny. Poland exploits concepts of its putative Exceptionalism also within the institutions of the EU and NATO in order to advance its national interests at Russia's expense.

Poland uses what it subjectively considers Russian Guilt to justify Polish Exceptionalism, thereby damaging Russia's soft power potential. (See: *Russian Guilt and Polish Exceptionalism* by Andrew Korybko, August 1, 2017 for more on the above)

Stepan Bandera In the Post-war

In such confusion, nationalism and Nazism flourished and men like Stepan Bandera and Adolf Hitler played their particular roles.

During the post-war of the late 1940s and early 50s, Stepan Bandera was an immigrant in West Germany. He worked for the BND, the German Intelligence Service, and its forerunner, the Gehlen Org, a top secret organization established in a Munich suburb run by Hitler's former intelligence chief in East Europe, General Reinhard Gehlen. Financed by the USA, the Gehlen Org specialized in espionage and training of spies to be infiltrated into the Soviet Union. Bandera and his wife, Yaroslava, and their three children had also settled in Munich. While the Germans and Americans used Bandera only sparingly and for many he seemed forgotten, the Soviet Union had not forgotten him. Repeated attempts were reportedly made on his life. Yet Bandera remained in Munich, living under the name of Stepan Popel, still a thorn in the side of his many enemies.

On October 15$^{th}$ of 1959, Bandera was killed at his apartment on Kreittmayrstrasse 7 in downtown Munich near the Main Rail Station, allegedly by the KGB assassin Bogdan Stashinsky. According to the police report Bandera had let his bodyguards off that day. When on the staircase Stashinsky raised a cyanide gun inside a rolled-up newspaper so that Bandera didn't have time to draw his own gun. Shot in the face, the fifty year-old Bandera died on a third-floor landing before an ambulance arrived. A medical examination established that the cause of his death was poison by cyanide gas. Stepan Bandera was buried in the Waldfriedhof Cemetery in Munich.

Bandera's murder was one of the most publicized assassinations of the Cold War. In the sensational show trial in 1962 in the Federal Constitutional Court in the city of Karlsruhe, the 30-year old alleged assassin , Bogdan Stashinsky, a self-declared Soviet citizen, was both defendant as well as star witness about the "nefarious" KGB. He allegedly defected to Germany together with his wife in 1961 and after spilling the beans to the CIA was handed over to German authorities. The young man was presented as a KGB killer and spy; he confessed to having assassinated another Ukrainian émigré in the 1950s. After weeks of testimony, Stashinsky—in reality a patsy—was condemned to only eight years in prison. For at least two assassinations! The whole affair stank to high heaven: of false flag operation.

Some reports claimed that the Bandera faction of the OUN had been backed by British MI6 since the 1930s. In any case Banderites were associated with CIA in the post-war for espionage in the Soviet Union. Yet American intelligence organizations too described Bandera as "extremely dangerous", traveling around in disguise, killer, counterfeiter and political kidnapper. When the Bavarian government cracked down, Bandera promptly offered his services to the German BND intelligence despite CIA's growing mistrust of him.

I fictionalized the Bandera-Stashinsky story in the political novel, *The Trojan Spy,* from which the following excerpts:

*Truth is elusive, many-sided. In any case a young Ukrainian KGB agent by the name of Stashinsky was later tried in Karlsruhe and convicted for the murder of Bandera with a poison spray concocted in Moscow. They said he was an agent of "Smersh".... A Russian acronym for Death To Spies. Once a top secret NKVD organization for its wet work. For the assassination of enemies. Killers all. Maybe they wanted to enlist him. But I doubt it. One said that during the Nazi occupation of the Ukraine, Stashinsky learned enough German to pass for a German and that he was hired by the KGB already at the age of nineteen after he was caught on a train without a ticket. All unlikely. Not KGB style. He admitted he worked in Germany.... He traveled around Germany.... He had a supervisor in Berlin.... But it's a long jump from that to Smersh. I've always suspected Ukrainian émigré political opponents of Bandera's murder. Ukrainian émigrés were always killing each other. With German and American help. That is, if Bandera was even murdered. He might have had a heart attack. As in a fairytale the cold-blooded assassin Stashinsky allegedly repented after he saw a newsreel in an East Berlin theater of poor Bandera lying in his coffin and his wife and children weeping. Can you imagine that touching scene? Oh, the soft heart of a KGB killer! ....Unimaginable....It's a ridiculous story from beginning to end. Not even the stuff of mythology. Who knows what really happened? Once he got back to East Berlin after killing Bandera, the handsome young Ukrainian fell head over heels in love with a German woman ... who hated the Soviet Union....When  she learned Stashinsky was a KGB agent, she convinced him of the perfidy of Communism and they escaped to West Germany the day before the Wall was built. Soap opera stuff. An American story, the whole Stashinsky affair. A Reader's Digest story. The naiveté is disgusting....*

Two feature films have been made about Stepan Bandera – *Assassination: An October Murder in Munich* (1995) and *The Undefeated* (2000), both directed by Oles Yanchuk—plus a number of documentary films.

# HERE I AM
### Remembrances of Meeting Cult Novelist Andrzej Kusniewicz

The Polish word, *jestem*—'I am', 'here I am', 'present'—defines the life of the writer and cult figure for a generation of Poles, Andrzej Kusniewicz. On an overcast pollution-infested Warsaw afternoon of over thirty years ago in his crowded study in a surprisingly bourgeois apartment in a quiet residential area of the capital city, the poet-novelist recalled the many occasions of his life when he answered with the word, *jestem*. During the course of our talk, I, the interviewer, came to recognize that he had earned a right to the word. For all his life he *had* been 'present'—so in contrast to the transitory nature of the past about which he wrote. "*Jestem*, I always answered when my parents called me—a Jewish child in Polish Galicia—for unusual tasks in unusual places in those most unusual of times." Kusniewicz answered 'present' when called to fight against the Nazi invaders of *Operation Barbarossa*. He was 'present' in the French *Resistence*. 'Present' in Mauthausen concentration camp. 'Present' in the Polish United Workers Party. 'Present' as a Polish Communist diplomat of the new post-World War II Poland. 'Present' as a writer in post-war Poland. When called to act, he answered: *jestem*. And his life presences were indeed many. Errant Quixote. Internal immigrant. Soldier. Resistance warrior. Death camp inmate. Communist. Diplomat. Poet. Novelist.

But today, end of the 1980s, stillness reigned in his life and he didn't seem like a cult figure at all. In those 1980s, people of Warsaw felt the uncertainties of the end of a period when familiar spaces were becoming less familiar. In those great spaces reaching from Russia to West Europe the sense of abandonment was perceptible: East European air was contaminated like that of Warsaw's conspiracy-infected air and power was changing hands. No wonder that people like Kusniewicz were lonely and their number accumulating, lonely people abandoned in familiar spaces that seemed lonely too. The uncertainty of social-political loneliness spread epidemically. Eastwards and westwards it spread while time itself seemed to be running out. Feelings of displacement mounted as invasive shape-shifting aliens infiltrated society. DNAs were mutating. Unaffiliated and traitorous leaders-presidents had declared war on the peoples abandoned in those unusual spaces so that people no longer knew who they were. Or where they were. People no longer counted as once. Engulfed by bushfire revolts running wild. Old vigils in the East tottered while artificial infections were hatched in the Western faraway. Pandemic change-renewal infected ancient spaces, contaminating its ancient abandoned peoples. Even nature was in rebellion. Gray skies hung low in the great lonely cities of Poland. Cities themselves were lonely. Pure air was found only high in the Carpathians, in the Alps, in the Urals, but people were confined to tight polluted spaces down below. Nature gives and nature takes away. Animal life was oblivious, nature neutral. Only faintly echoed lonely voices like that of Andrzej Kusniewicz.

"Nationality has always been an enigma for me," Kusniewicz said. "Today I'm Polish, I write Polish, I think in Polish. It might seem settled. But is it?" Which was his country? he wondered. Ukrainian East Galicia? Polish West Galicia? Russia? Austria? Nationality could change overnight in the dynamic of the East Europe of his earlier days. You could go to bed in one country and wake up in another. Nationality mutated like a virus. Such change symbolizes the time ending atmosphere pervading the writer's works.

The 1980s were confusing times. Neither foreign observers nor participants understood what was happening in the expanses of Poland, while immense things were happening that would change all of East Europe. Change the world. In 1980, Lech Walesa (Lech, the name of the founder of Poland a millennium ago), an electrician-trade unionist in the Lenin Shipyards of Gdansk in northern Poland, had organized Solidarnosc, a free trade union in opposition to the Communist government in

Warsaw led by General Wojciech Jaruzelski, one of the liberators of Poland from the Nazi grip. Solidarnosc had the solid backing of a powerful man and institution: Karol Wojtyla from Krakow, then known as Pope John Paul II, tough but widely loved boss of the Roman Catholic Church in Rome. Devout Catholics forever, those Poles! And now Solidarnosc, the mortal enemy of Communism, had their man in Rome who dedicated his Papacy to undermining the foundations of world Communism in Moscow. And the unexpected was on its way like a hell-bent destiny: in 1985 the new General Secretary of the Soviet Communist Party, Mikhail Gorbachev, launched his program of *glasnost* and *perestroika* (openness and restructuring) headed pell-mell toward social democracy and free-market capitalism and the savage rape of Russia in the 1990s. We can see now what earlier was cloudy: Walesa and Solidarnosc, Wojtyla and the Vatican and Washington were right on schedule. Operation Overthrow was underway, in the Vatican, in Washington, in Poland ... thirty-four years before the Maidan Nazi takeover in neighboring Ukraine. The sequence of events leading to the spread of Fascism today is portentous, its rhythm lethal: 1980-Solidarnosc; 1989 –the dissolution of the Soviet Union; 2014-a U.S.-managed Nazi coup in Ukraine.

But it is turning out to be a Pyrrhic victory for Washington. In the end a powerful Russia re-emerged and the USA began its decline as did the Austro-Hungarian Empire, an incident of which decline Andrzej Kusniewicz depicts in his novel, *Lesson in a Dead Language* of 1977.

Kusniewicz, who in those times had retired to his ivory tower of memories now said with a sigh that it was inevitable that he thought historically. "We East Europeans have a lot of it to deal with. We are living history. But I do write poetically, it seems." And I read in the work of the poet and novelist how he combined history and his memories in a way that made him the great writer he was. He wrote about other times as seen through his poet's binoculars and from his memories he fashioned books for films.

Although I have forgotten details of the real him, I sometimes think of Andrzej Kusniewicz. And I hear his soft Polish pronunciation of *jestem.* I remember vividly how we sat quietly in his abandoned space in which he too seemed abandoned and alone in the world. All the others were gone. All was in the past that he searched and recovered in his works. Cold brown walls lined by framed black and white photographs of past matters pressed against us. Desk, typewriter, mounds of papers, newspaper articles, handwritten notes stuck here and there, double rows of books in shelves, stacks of books tottering in corners. Books in Polish, German, Russian, Ukrainian, English, French, Italian.

"My languages", he said, sadness in his tone. "But I don't know for certain which is mine."

Backtrack seventy years from the late 1980s Warsaw to the setting woven into his novel, *Lesson in a Dead Language.* In *Lekcja Martwego Jezyka* Kusniewicz relates the past … and his memories of it. Like looking at the past, at memories, through binoculars. The past remains the past, alive only in memory. And the future, dark and uncertain. We are in the last year of World War I, in Galicia crushed between Poland and Ukraine. The past flashes past in Kusniewicz's *Lesson*, with little dialogue, many sentences beginning with 'and' or 'while' in Polish, his frequent references back to something cloudy that happened in the past. Memory.

His imaginary Lieutenant Kiekeritz, slowly dying of tuberculosis, is as fixated on his fever as he is fixed in his epoch. Every day at three p.m. his fever arrived on his thermometer, 37°, or even 38. Then went back down to almost normal. And again during the night it rose and it fell. Up and down. Measured with his thermometer.

In the field hospital the Regimental doctor: "All this thermometer maneuvering irritates and exasperates you. So why not just send it to the devil? How does this constant measuring help you?"

The Lieutenant stopped taking his temperature and thinking about his health in general—he got better. His non-measured temperature, offended, gave up and surrendered.

Another doctor had advised him to take his temperature three times a day, and not under his arm but in the anus. In order to really know. "Does where interest you so much, Herr Doctor?" the ironic Lieutenant Kiekeritz asked.

"Well, no, or rather yes. It should interest us both," the good doctor said. "Since I'm here to treat and cure you."

"Ok, treat me, that's your profession, maybe also your pleasure, I don't know. But cure me? You like to joke, Herr Doctor."

Always subtle and suggestive, Kusniewicz, in that East European way. Kusniewicz's rhythm and Kiekeritz' illness and death run in parallel with the illness and decline and death of the Hapsburg Monarchy. The writer did not even have to invent his character; he found him in place, molded by the declining Empire. The Lieutenant's cynicism inhered in him, as did the disorder and confusion of his existence lost there in the mountains so far from a center, yet so near, the generalized degeneration of the dying monarchy of which he was distractedly and carelessly aware. He was living in a disaster. The Lieutenant's tuberculosis was his personal disaster which he was able to observe clinically ... but with a certain dark humor. His temperature rising and falling and finally rising again personifies the sinking multiethnic empire, invisible but omnipresent. The disastrous reality of his times was harsh, which Kusniewicz does not ignore. A brief flash would stun Lieutenant Kiekeritz, like an epiphany, then vanish into nothingness.

A typical Kusniewicz description of life and nature in the novel, *Lesson in a Dead Language*:
*The end of World War I is near. On the margin of history in a hamlet of the Carpathian Mountains. Lieutenant Kiekeritz is supposed to care for his tuberculosis corroded lungs but in reality he knows he faces an ineluctable death. Time of a last season, in a sumptuous and wild mountain landscape life deploys its pageantry*

*for him, offering his refined sensitivity exacerbated by the illness the perfumed cocktails and the rarest of colors. That is the décor which death needs in order to appear as if its ugliness were the secret accomplice of so much beauty.*

*A grotesque death, absurd, of which the Lieutenant is aware, observing its ever more precise manifestations with a mixture of detachment and fascination. On his solitary walks and insomniac nights peopled by dreams and memories, he establishes with it a strange hide-and-seek game in which the reader, spellbound, in his turn enters. Under his eyes is woven a tight skein of correspondences, forebodings, warnings. Death embroils the tracks, jumbles the cards, hides its face behind that of the goddess Diane or the gypsy performing at the Colombus Circus, before finally appearing in the guise of a pure and defaced young girl. Around the Lieutenant evolve other beings, picturesque and binding, carried there by the hazards of the war and destiny, and ignorant of the drama in act.*

The reader finds in *Lesson in a Dead Language* an original meditation about art and the times, about the destiny of the living substance and of that which one calls, erroneously, the *inanimate*. Objects for collection only, like Kiekeritz's sudden attraction to a bad, dusty print of a *Salomé*. You find all the characteristics of the immense talent of Kusniewicz: an allusive but omnipresent sensuality, magnificent descriptions of nature, all marked by an innovative writing, rich and savory, the writing of a poet.

*Slowly walking through the grass, which brings one up to the pass revealed or hiding from the bend in an alley, a pleasure garden, a lawn. Plates-bands of flowers. Fragments of unexpected landscapes, all totally unreal, in distant blue skies. A pond, almost a lake. Small benches in the shade of huge trees. Monuments and gazebos. Arbors. We could, without changing anything, encapsulate all this in a fine gold frame and hang it on the wall, a watercolor; this would make a very beautiful period picture, picturesque and a little nostalgic...*

Andrzej Kusniewicz (born 1904 in Polish Galicia-died 1993 in Warsaw) falls into the category of European novelists who dealt with the era of the decline and demise of the Austro-Hungarian Empire, coinciding with the end of the Great War, World War I. The better known and widely popular in the German-speaking world, Joseph Roth, also from Polish Galicia and ten years older than Kusniewicz, wrote the famous novel, *Radetsky March* of 1932, which also chronicles the decline and fall of the Empire. And *the* Empire it was: Austria and Hungary, and Czech Republic, Slovakia, Slovenia, Croatia, Bosnia, and parts of Poland, Romania, Italy, Ukraine, Serbia, Montenegro, Moldova. Many reasons for the Great War are to be found in that list of peoples and in the clash among their overlapping languages, cultures, faiths and interests and in their distances one from the other.

However, Kusniewicz's style is more subtle and complex, more labyrinthine than that of *der rote Roth* (the red Roth). A fellow man of the Left, Roth was the great journalist of the era, a kind of European John Reed. The prose of both Roth and Kusniewicz exudes a charm arising not only from the sunset of an empire and nostalgia for times past, but from a Proustian recovery of a lost past which displays both the dying empire's brilliance and its fragility and, in the case of Kusniewicz, an incomparable sensuality.

As a result, his *Lesson in a Dead Language* became a popular film in 1979. Directed by a major Polish cinema figure, Janusz Majewski, the film story depicts tubercular Lieutenant Kiekeritz in a sanatorium in the Carpathian Mountains searching for a meaning in life by collecting works of art that he can leave as a legacy, a film profoundly marked by the motif of death, the Austrian officer's own and that of an empire. For Majewski, it was retro cinema, a sentimental journey to the recent past and traditions of former Mitteleuropa. A journey into the cultural mix of that part of Europe, most of which was the former Austro-Hungarian Empire, to which the filmmaker then added more flavors of the bitterness of the awareness of time passing: Kiekeritz's preparation for death as a metaphor of a dying age and culture.

In those years Polish poets saw the realization of Dostoevsky's vision of European culture sinking in stages into inhumanity. The end of that empire was the end of European culture. Its religion, art, philosophy had been only a façade, as seen again today in 2021 as Europe disintegrates in dissension, nationalism and egoism, the heavy hand of U.S. imperialism, and enticing invitations to turn its head to the East.

A long list of writers—poets and novelists, historians and journalists—have made Polish letters great, not only in that historical period, but also still today as well as centuries earlier: Joseph Conrad, Adam Mickiewicz, Isaac Deutscher, Czeslaw Milosz (Nobel poet, 1980), Witold Dombrowicz, Gustaw Herling-Grudzinski,, Jaroslaw Iwaszkiewicz, Isaac Bashevis Singer, Henrik Sienkiewicz, Wislawa Szymborska (Nobel poetess, 1996) , Adam Zagajewski.

Kusniewicz's Lieutenant Kiekeritz died his tubercular death at the same time the Austro-Hungarian Empire died. Soldiers changed the emblems on their hats from the Empire's colors to diverse national colors of the dead empire. Only history and memories remained. Kusniewicz died in 1993 and was buried in the Military Cemetery in Warsaw. I think the ghosts of Poland's great poets must be bitterly disappointed in the extreme right-wing Poland of today.

# THE GEHLEN ORGANIZATION AND CIA

In February 2019 Germany opened a brand new intelligence complex in the city of Berlin. The headquarters of the BND (Bundesnachrichtendienst or Federal Intelligence Service) occupies a huge space—much as STASI or State Security Service once did in East Berlin the former German Democratic Republic—and is said to employ a total of over six thousand persons. The move from its former secret location in the Munich suburb of Pullach reflects both the centralization in the capital of federal institutions that after World War Two were widely dispersed throughout Germany and the country's efforts to veil the nation's Nazi past. The BND location in Germany's capital city is also a giant step away from the obsessive secrecy of its former location in Munich, hidden away in an obscure suburb, operating under a cover name and above all until the late 1950s in effect an affiliate of the CIA. The move to Berlin can be interpreted also as the BND's declaration of sovereignty which, however, it decidedly has not achieved, no more than is Germany itself a sovereign state.

The BND dates back to its formation in 1956 when it replaced the CIA-sponsored affiliate, known (or rather largely unknown), as the Gehlen Organization, named after its creator, the German East European specialist, the former Nazi Lieutenant General Reinhard Gehlen. In the immediate post-war period, Gehlen Org, as it was called in intelligence parlance, zeroed in on Soviet-dominated East Europe. Gehlen Org's operations were financed by the CIA and staffed by hundreds of Gehlen's own Nazi intelligence staff and former SS men who were conveniently released—and denazification be damned—from West European internment camps to join Gehlen's first headquarters in the Spessart Mountains in central Germany. Since American intelligence of the immediate post-war period knew little about the Soviet Union, ultra-top secret Gehlen Org was the CIA's eyes and ears throughout East Europe.

A look at the figure of Reinhard Gehlen and his organization and its relationship with the CIA is worthwhile since to a certain extent he and his SS men established early post-war policies of the USA vis-à-vis its erstwhile ally, the Soviet Union … policies which have remained largely intact today. His staff was composed of Nazis, many of whom Gehlen would have known, directly or indirectly. When the former General's staff swelled to some three thousand persons his Gehlen Org was transferred to a twenty-five acre compound in Munich-Pullach where it operated under the innocuous name of South German Industrial Development Organization. By the early fifties Gehlen Org was said to employ some four thousand intelligence specialists in Germany and a like number of undercover agents throughout Eastern Europe … especially in East Germany where their very shadowy presence justified STASI severity and cast doubts on the spontaneity of the East German workers' uprising in 1953. Gehlen's activities consisted of the infiltration of secret agents into East European countries, espionage, analysis and the laying of policy guidelines for the CIA. Evidently Gehlen agents played roles in the 1956 revolt in Hungary the events in Prague in 1968 and Poland in 1980 and most certainly in the dissolution of Yugoslavia. Thus Gehlen's activities in East Europe in those years show that Cold War was not only propaganda; it was also invisible boots on the ground war.

The CIA-Gehlen secret link is one of the most disturbing examples of the U.S. close relationship with Nazism and Nazi Germany dating back to the formative period of Hitlerian Nazism in the early 1920s. Few people know even the name "Gehlen". Yet he and his SS men not only indoctrinated the newborn CIA but determined and led American post-war activities in East Europe, and, in a special way, conditioned U.S. policies toward the Soviet Union and Russia today.

Historiography has shown examples of the vast American economic assistance to the young Nazi movement in Munich from 1919-1920, which many U.S. planners saw as a future force to crush Soviet Communism against which the USA along with

Great Britain and France had been intervening militarily in Eastern Russia since 1917. As far as America's day-to-day working collaboration with German Nazism is concerned, silence has been the rule. Moreover, as discussed in the introductory article above denazification after Nazi Germany's defeat was a joke. It simply never happened. Anyone who spent time in Germany even a decade or so after the end of WWII heard right and left the refrain of older, non-denazified Germans and high-ranking American military: "America and Germany together to crush the Soviet Union!"

What kind of a man was Reinhard Gehlen? (born April 3, 1902 in Erfurt, died June 8, 1979 in Munich-Starnberg). Gehlen, the German military intelligence man, German nationalist ... and traitor. Both he and General Friedrich Paulus were traitors although their destinies were vastly different. Paulus found a place in Moscow; Gehlen found his in Washington. Gehlen, conspirator and liar. Man of light and dark. Man of the day and the night. Both Führer loyal and a traitor long before Hitler fired him ... perhaps truly for incompetence. Gehlen, fake Nazi, opportunist, administrative bungler and nepotist, naive dabbler but also East European expert. All these things in his seventy-seven years. Yet he was destined to become President of the BND, apparently thanks to the CIA and also to his friendship with Konrad Adenauer, first Chancellor of the post-war German Federal Republic.

In any case, to American beginners the schemer Reinhard Gehlen appeared as a brilliant expert in intelligence matters. He was highly praised also in Nazi Germany as he worked his way up through the military ranks, finally reaching the General status. But generalship did not satiate Gehlen's ambitions. Most anyone with sufficient tenacity could become a general. It was like a big club of gentlemen, and Gehlen was neither. He wanted much more. From the start he strove for something of his very own ... with no one over him. An appealing quality to the early CIA that desired the same. Yet there are doubts whether the CIA ever completely mastered and controlled Gehlen. In any case, Operation

Barbarossa—the invasion of Russia—was the chance of a lifetime for the enterprising Gehlen. He was a military intelligence man whose ambition to have his own intelligence organization was realized when during the war he took over the Wehrmacht Foreign Armies East (*Fremde Heere Ost* or FHO) military intelligence service in Eastern Europe, a parallel intelligence gathering organization, separate from the regular army's *Abwehr*. He was the recognized expert. The boss. Except for the Führer—whom he bamboozled as he later must have the CIA—his hands were free. So it was no surprise that his information gradually began to differ from that of the Abwehr. His intelligence had the Gehlen stamp— true, false, ambivalent ... whatever best fitted the occasion.

William T. Vollmann in his previously cited novel about Germany and Russia and World War Two, *Europe Central*, offers examples of Gehlen's wartime reporting. When General Paulus's Sixth Army was surrounded by Russian armies at Stalingrad and began methodically crushing everything inside the encirclement, Gehlen's Fremde *Heere Ost* reassured Paulus and Hitler that "the enemy troop concentrations remained much too weak for far-reaching operations." Cynicism or incompetence? Then while the Sixth Army of 300,000 German soldiers was being decimated and Paulus's last Panzer tanks had been lost, Gehlen sent him old air reconnaissance photographs in which there was no indication at all of Soviet troop movements. Then when in the cellars of besieged Stalingrad the horse steak rations were ending even for the top German officers, Gehlen's *Fremde Heers Ost* reported that "the situation of Stalingrad might very well be serious". Then— ah, that sly and unpredictable Gehlen!—while the German part of Stalingrad was falling and Paulus about to surrender, Gehlen briefed the Führer that "a powerful enemy tank attack was repelled after a temporary break-in" and "enemy artillery fire was strengthening", "there is enemy pressure on our positions" and "enemy advances on many fronts", mild reports that denied the reality of defeat which however sufficed to infuriate the Führer. Gehlen's increasingly pessimistic reports displeased the Führer to the degree that before war's end he fired him. But Gehlen was never one to be caught with his pants down. He always had a plan B or more backups as needed. Those misleading reports concerning Stalingrad indicate he had planned far ahead. During the war years he collected an enormous quantity of intelligence on the Soviet Union and on the precious Soviet Order of Battle, which he stored in water-tight drums and buried in secret places in Austria. Then like others he let himself and his trusted aids be captured by the American Counter Intelligence Corps (CIC), where a warm welcome awaited him.

In 1945, the gap in U.S. intelligence about its former ally and new enemy, the Soviet Union, was abysmal. Russia! Communists! Soviet Union! Why all the talk about Stalingrad? Who knows where Smolensk or Kursk are? Who speaks their crazy languages or knows what the taiga is? Few American military men knew anything about those boundless expanses and enigmatic peoples in the East reaching nearly to America. Meanwhile, back at home, Soviet studies blossomed overnight in American academia, an indication that the anti-Soviet spirit was a long-term affair; the military itself began training first hundreds, then thousands of recruits in the languages of East Europe. And to the degree that anti-Soviet and anti-Russian propaganda intensified, the mood of the American public quickly became anti-Soviet and anticommunist. The Cold War was revving up on all fronts. The U.S. wartime OSS intelligence regrouped and in 1947 was reborn as the CIA and Reinhard Gehlen was one of its cornerstones; some observers go so far as to consider him a co-founder of the Central Intelligence Agency. Reinhard Gehlen, the man of light and dark, offered his precious intelligence treasures about America's great enemy in the East. And he offered also the services of those hundreds of Nazi German East European specialists in his retinue.

In retrospect, Gehlen's role in U.S. intelligence—as far as the Soviet Union in the first ten post-war years is concerned—appears as a case of the tail wagging the dog. The CIA hired Gehlen and his people who then taught them what Soviet Russia was all about. Oh, yes, the U.S. Embassy in Moscow functioned, but what did it know about the nitty-gritty of its Soviet ally's military operations. Gehlen knew, he had to know, that his time was limited as the CIA developed and grew. And also its patience with his ways was limited. So Gehlen worked fast. And his hands were everywhere in the defeated and destroyed Germany. One said that every German prisoner of war returnee from Soviet internment was processed by Gehlen … like being interrogated by the SS. But also by American military intelligence organizations, many of which behind the scenes were managed by the Gehlen Org in Munich. Why? Because the Germans knew the right questions to ask.

In such an atmosphere of power struggles—even though among like-minded people—clashes of interest were inevitable. All the while, secretive, ambiguous Gehlen was contriving his German future, which was realized in 1956 when he became the first President of the Federal Intelligence Service, (BND).The CIA controlled the Gehlen Org and the still fictitious country of Germany itself and it controlled also the BND, just not as tightly as it had Gehlen Org in the decade before. And most certainly there is another CIA-BND within the BND, and another within it. The CIA and the Gehlen BND seem to have gradually settled into a Big Brother—Little Brother relationship. We may assume it remains the same in the U.S. occupied, non-sovereign Federal Republic of Germany today that is straining at the leashes toward a new relationship with its old foe, Russia. Though Hitler's Nazi Party opposed Russia as much as it did Communism, the relationship between the two countries, Germany and Russia, has long been marked by love, hate and envy. The two countries have too many common interests to stay forever apart. When—and if— Nord Stream 2 opens, Russian gas will effect untold change in the Russian role in Europe. And ironically German-Russian relations will set the tone for those changes.

# WORDS UNSPOKEN

## A Short Fiction

# Foreword

Many historians perceive of history as a determining force that individual lives merely illustrate but as far as my own attempts at fiction about reality are concerned, I agree only partially. Although pieces of history and much "place" decorate my fiction—often called historical fiction—my major attention goes to fictional people who, I believe, make history not only true but also realistic. Fictional personae illustrate not only what people of the real-world experience but show what they feel, the turmoil and conflicts that real people experience in their daily lives. History presents the facts. Fiction offers the reality for which most fiction writers strive. Fiction writers can reconstruct events as well as historians but also put real people in imaginary situations in a way historians cannot. Fred Weinstein in his *History and Theory* writes that while non-fiction gives you the facts, fiction gives you the truth. History tells you what happened; fiction tells you how it felt. So readers must wonder where history ends and fiction begins.

Moreover, pure history also has its limits. As in the example of the aftermath of war, there is no getting around the reality that the victors write the history of what has happened, their versions of history. Yet both the victors and the defeated are living people, not just inanimate objects. Only in the very long term of the great sweep of the history of epochs can people be reduced to mere illustrators of history. After all, conquerors like Napoleon believed that 'history is the tale of the victors'. Decades ago I was fixated on the determining role of 'historic Rome'; today, as I come to know the historical significance of my adoptive home city, Rome emerges as proof that "pure" historicism has no heart. How can it have a heart when, as Walter Benjamin reminds us in confirmation of Napoleon, *"It marches with the victors."* While the history that people have lived challenges the imaginative capacity of historians to account for it, it is fiction that offers the heterogeneity and discontinuity that history written by historians cannot. (Weinstein)

Most novelists agree that fiction in general offers true, real and realistic  history: Gore Vidal, Saul Bellow, E.L. Doctorow, Graham Greene, Norman Mailer, John Dos Passos, Robert Musil, Günther Grass, Carlos Fuentes, et al, believe that only fiction can bring readers closer to the subjective perceptions of people in history. As Nicola Chiaromonte writes in *Paradox of History*: *Only in fiction and the imaginary can we learn something real about individual experience.* [1]The title of this novella, *Words Unspoken*, occurred to me before I wrote one word of the text. I was reading a novel when suddenly, apropos of nothing, these two words popped into my head: Words Unspoken. Words Unspoken. The two words remained fixed in my mind. Nevertheless, I too later wondered why these words as the title for a work of fiction. Though the title *Words Unspoken* rings peculiar, as I got used to the title's words I became cognizant of just how many words in our lives do remain unspoken, dark and untellable like some of our own acts, or acts of those we love and admire. Some things *are* but will never be known unless they are revealed in words. But not everything that occurs to us that can be reproduced in words can be actually spoken. Perhaps only alone in the desert can you speak all those words that must remain unspoken in our daily lives.

I had been thinking of a story set in post-war Germany where I lived from the years when the immediate post-war period was just ending. I had tampered mentally with a story about the return home from the Russian front of a German veteran at the end of World War Two. My story, *Words Unspoken*, would begin with the returnee's leap into the frenetic atmosphere of a destroyed Germany. At that time I received as a gift the wonderful eight hundred-page, historical novel, *Europe Central*, by William T. Vollmann, concerning chiefly Germany and Russia, two countries at the center of my literary interests. Had I not read that book first, my story would have been different.

I have attempted in these three stories to depict with historical fiction a small part of the *sweep* of history from the battle of Stalingrad in 1942-43, through the Cold War, and until the collapse of East European Communist governments in 1989. The one story I had in mind became three, which plus selected historical facts combined to form this novella. In this story a small number of persons illustrate—in a limited manner— that tightly packed half century of history: the finals years of World War Two, the division of both Germany and Europe itself into two parts, the creation of NATO and the European Union in West Europe and the Warsaw Pact in East Europe, the Korean War, the explorations in space of the USSR and the USA, the Vietnam wars, the fall of Communist-led governments of East Europe, the US/NATO wars against Yugoslavia.

Simultaneously with these and other world-shaking events, also occurred the great *swerve* of the post-WWII United States of America during which people of the USA, Europe and the entire world became aware that everything, every aspect of life had rapidly changed from what it once was. This was the period of the *bestialization* of American Corporatist Capitalism. So today the realities of very real people of our own times who have experienced these bewildering events crammed into such a restricted period can easily be depicted. But it is in the fiction of writers like those mentioned above where the reality of that swerve emerges most clearly.

# PART TWO: THE POWERS OF LOVE AND WAR

Stalingrad. Stalingrad. Stalingrad changed everything in Helmut Seifert Hartmann's life. Since his return home from the war Helmut had not felt emotions of normal human warmth, none of the personal kindliness he had expected. Instead of warmth and healing he felt only chaos in the post-war atmosphere, something almost otherworldly but still much as it had seemed in Russia. He was aware that the very ugliness of his experiences had changed him too in that he still felt war and fire and death and the smells of war in his every breath. To returnees like him the everlasting peace politicians spoke of meant little. He was just a war-shattered, sex-hungry survivor from the war in East Europe where among the young men inhabiting the cellars of the German-occupied part of Stalingrad cold and rats and smells had reigned. Ach, the smells. *Zapach voyny*, the smell of war, he repeated as he often had in Russian. Nights. In the cellars of Stalingrad. Today, it was in the dark corners of the homeland that he sought the fire of life. [2]

At the same time the shortage of men at home had created the pain of loneliness for German women …women alone and lonely but each harboring love to share … and no men to whom to give it. The men had all been far away on a front somewhere. And few were the men who returned home whole. Human relations in Helmut's view were as incomprehensibly convoluted as his in the cellars in the East together with the cold ragged soldiers and the insatiable rats and the familiar smells of war.

Things had gone haywire in Central Europe. War costs everyone early, he told himself. Russia was devastated. And war had ravaged the homeland as it did all of Europe; the whole continent was in irreparable shambles. The stench of charred wood and crushed stone of the bombed-out cities permeated his confusing life … his earthly existence itself. Like all soldiers he noted that special thing about total war: the smells. War had its particular smells, smells that in the rest of his life, he knew, would never be smothered.

Nonetheless, in the post-war life in the cellars of the demolished cities of the unrecognizable homeland the unbounded urge for life precipitated into frenetic promiscuity infecting men and women alike … and flowered to the steady beat of flowing beer and schnapps. Stalingrad was dank, dark and cold cellars and cold men. And the ubiquitous rats. Rats smelling the men's blood. Huge, dirty rats. Rats crawling over him in the cold endless night. And now back home too lived life bloomed in the cold cellars. As did the rats. As in Russia, the above ground of the homeland was destroyed, but life still beckoned. Full of drink and lust for life, time and again he and one or the other of the lonely women threw themselves into the sparse grass behind one drinking hole or the other … into the wild wild grass. One into the other. Men and women without names hungry for the fire of life reunited.

'Me! Who walked back from the East Front! I made it back. I got back whole. A whole man. Today, at home again, I walk across Munich's Viktualienmarkt and Marienplatz as if on display. I'm in demand. As if all the other men had fallen in Stalingrad. And here we're starting over again.' No need to attack the world again. Helmut vowed to adopt a new strategy as well as a new heart to replace the sad and desolate surviving one. Cling, cling with all your might to the new and to love nearly lost but which he knew was immortal. One history had concluded; a new one opened like daffodils in spring. Life was not over. Not yet. Dreams kept him alive. Dreams that never expired. For memory remained. Memory of bygone dreams spawning nascent hope of a new beginning. Better than the acceptance of nonexistence, the death of emotions and permanent exile.

In Munich like elsewhere the lonely women and scarce men created a volatile situation of morbid rapture. Five years of unleashed rapture. Short years. Eternal years.

The sick rapture would never end, I thought then.

Until Ute came into my life. From the start I loved her name. Ute. A meaningful name. Of constancy, intransigence and perseverance, like a deep and steady current in the dark waters of the Black Sea, a current unaffected by surface turbulence. Qualities not in great demand in the period of irrepressible frenzy for life, a time when personal willfulness was truly truant. Like the military sniper in Stalingrad says before he pulls the trigger: It's nothing personal. I had learned what that meant. But Ute put an end to that impersonal life: she was the new German woman.

I entered the Alter Wirt for a beer. It was just another place in this Munich suburb I called Grünwaldgrad. But as always I was looking for someone. She was sitting at the table just opposite mine. We looked at each other. Currents tinged with the unknown and sensuality passed from one to the other. Her short dark hair, the smoothness of her face untouched by make-up made her different in every way. She was alone. Hardly a surprise. I had learned that every aloneness is similar in its loneliness. In a Stalingrad cellar, a Munich basement club, or in the Alter Wirt beer hall. I knew that the beautiful woman sitting opposite me knew aloneness.

It's Saturday afternoon in a late Munich summer. My day off. I carry two beers to her table. She smiles at me. Few words are spoken. Mere pleasantries. Unnecessary words remain unsaid. After a while I suggest a walk, a *Spaziergang* along the banks of the Isar. Munich summers are so short. We should take advantage of it. But Ute wants to go to Schwabing. So *Zum wohl!* We drink up. And off to downtown we go.

Marienplatz is in *Trümmerhaufen*. The tram ride through the ruins and rubble of a once great city quotes the cost of war. Words are unnecessary. Frauenkirche, our Notre Dame, the shell of a symbol hanging over it all. Main street leading to the Stachus is a mere passageway cleared of rubble and lined by ghastly ghostly shells of the city's gutted churches, The *Hofgarten* is just a façade, the silhouette of the remaining half. The dome of the former Army Museum juts up in the mist behind it. The Siegestor—the Victory Gate—sags in defeat.

The empty shells of the 'Thousand Year Reich!' about which we joked in the cellars of Stalingrad. A thousand years and never again a thousand, our philosopher quoted Nostradamus. Yet already at the end of the first winter in Russia the soldiers felt the end. Moscow and Leningrad had not fallen ... would never fall. German soldiers perceived defeat rushing toward them like a troika in flames. And Russians felt it too. Russians always knew it ... had always known it. Just a matter of time, they thought ... and the Russian winter.

The tram stops right in front of my favorite Leopoldgastätte. The place itself a survivor too, a relic of the past. *Gott sei Dank*. Ute and I, Munich beer and Steinhäger. *Zum wohl*! Chugalug. Ute hardly blinks. We sit at my usual table near a big window facing Leopoldstrasse. My necessity. I fear the shadows of rear tables recalling dark cold cellars, rats and the stink of war.

Ute tells me about her home. The swinging swaying suspension railway—the *Schwebebahn*—runs up the Wupper Valley toward Düsseldorf, flying over the ruins of the industrial Ruhr. An air train. The transport system of the future ... until the day they transported a smallish elephant in it. It fell into the River Wupper ... but the *Schwebebahn* remained like a Futurist Installation.

I tell her about Stalingrad cellars and how they flew me out with the last transport from the encircled Sixth Army. General Paulus and 240,000 soldiers stayed behind. Then they surrendered.

"But I broke through," I whisper. "Like a Galapagos turtle, I made it through. Back to German lines."

"Why you, do you think? And not other baby turtles? Chance?"

"Military intelligence was my job. The *Abwehr*. Too valuable to leave me there for captivity. After making me talk the Russians would shoot me like they did the SS men who'd tortured and killed their people. And I didn't know anything of interest to reveal. That would make the torture worse."

"Now you're here ... a hero. You made it back."

"I'm not a hero. I just made it back. I walked to the West, Ute. But I stopped on the Elbe. And together with the remainders of our armies—with the old men and the boys—I fell back. And back and back. Until it was over. I made it through to the Amis. Got through again. They sent us POWs to America. Picked beans in North Carolina until they sent me back home. Back to München. I've always been lucky. Nearly always."

"It kills me how you always made it through. Turtle man! And now? Why in Grünwald?"

"Got a job across the river. Electrical company!"

"Pullach, eh? The spy nest. Gehlen! Everybody knows that. Or they know and don't know. Ah, those spies! Late for spies now, no?"

"Never too late ... for spies, is it?"

"I read a film résumé that would interest you. The Gehlen Org story. Someone killed it while the two pages still lay on my desk. There one day, gone the next. Top secret."

"Top secret, yes! Gehlen Org is another Ami plot!"

The Fräulein brings us more beer and Steinhäger. Smiles at us. Lovingly. It was always in the air at the Leopoldgastätte. Sex ... and echoes of loves we once knew.

Ute Friedrich is a light-haired *Rheinländerin* of twenty-six years. Were she a man, she would still be a Prussian pig for Bavarians. But since she is a beautiful woman, she is instead an *Ausländerin*, a foreigner. She says she feels neither. Her family had been well-to-do before the war. Property holdings in the Wupper Valley and interests in Düsseldorf. Well-off. When her father didn't return from the war, her mother gradually sold off property so that their lifestyle remained about the same, providing Ute a Schwabing apartment while she studied Germanistic at Munich University. Now she lives in München-Pullach with a three-year old daughter and is a screen writer at Bavarian Film Studio in Grünwald-Geiselgasteig.

"Gehlen and Pullach seem to link us," she says. (3)

"Link us? Does Pullach have something to do with it? Pullach is just a place?" "Silly! Of the link we both feel … one to the other."

"How are we linked, Ute? You have your life. You, a well-to-do career woman from the Rheinland, a film writer. And me, a Sudeten German from the cellars of Stalingrad. Are we linked? By Gehlen and Pullach?"

"Cynic! I meant the war. Gehlen and evil and the war. And Stalingrad cellars. All that made you different. You don't get out of such things unscathed."

"Unscathed! Certainly not. But Gehlen's not the point."

Careful, Helmut Hartmann! Links are links, so don't ruin this because of my proclivity to pardon Gehlen personally just because he too had betrayed the Nazis who had destroyed my generation. Several generations … only to make even greater concessions to his own egomaniacal opportunism and maybe to a greater evil in his will to power. His *Wille zur Macht*. Ute knows the truth. She knows Major General Gehlen sold out everything to the Amis. Although the transformation from sanity to madness of our generation was swift, the change back to sanity is an endless process. Civilian life is not easy either.

"You know what I mean! An all-important *what*. Gehlen and Pullach mean cynicism. And it can make you incapable of love. Real love. We forgive too much in our times, don't you think, Helmut? We forgive the Nazis. We the German people forgive ourselves."

"Ute! Please. *Ich bitte dich*."

I hear the forlorn tone in my own voice. The despair that she's right even though we both seem to feel enjoined to follow our instincts to let ourselves be enveloped in the succor of … of nascent love. So for a while we sit quietly, both of us thinking, thinking, thinking. Thinking of how things might have been. People do that often in these times: think of how things might have been. We sip our now stale beers, awkward and in uneasy indecisiveness. And casting surreptitious glances one at the other as if real love in these post-war-torn times were something unprecedented. Or something undeserved. Or danger itself.

On the tram back to Grünwald she tells me about her relationship with another student at the university. An American! By chance, he was an Ami. At twenty she was pregnant. But he never knew. He left her life and never knew his daughter. And now we *are* speaking of love. Yes, I was thinking of the love so lacking in my life. Signs of our times. After the mayhem everybody is subconsciously looking for love. One of the few real life values left. The only way back to normality … to normality after the brief glories of conquest and occupation of Europe to our cellar lives of impending defeat under the ponderous buildings of Stalingrad in the East … and the eternity in the cellars of our newly destroyed world at home. The normality that seemed unobtainable after a life imagined by madmen. A life built on unjustified illusions, then dismantled on the tremors of ravaged hopes … and which for many terminated in their irremediable death wishes.

But Ute knows the answers. She's never forgotten love and selflessness and the power to transcend tragedy.

Back again in the Alter Wirt in Grünwald. Coffee and Weinbrand on the table. An east wind has come up outside. Cold is coming. My cigarette lighter flicks a nervous flame. It always works. Thirty times in a row. It could do a hundred times straight. In the cold cellars of Russia we competed. Winner takes all. My Zippo always won. Won what? A slice of horse meat at the most … or maybe rat meat.

"How did you get into all that?"

"All that what? You keep saying that."

"Gehlen's Intelligence. The turtle that got through?"

"I was Sudetendeutsch until they resettled many of us in Germany. So many of us here that we called it Münchenbad … after your Karlsbad. I always knew the spa by its Czech name."

I think: 'Maybe it saved me too … to meet Ute Friedrich.'

I digress to the spa just to postpone love talk and to try to say something sensible to a normal German woman. Karlsbad or Karlovy Vary, as if that name were something to clutch at and cling to for a generation that went wrong.

"I called it Karlovy Vary as I learned it in elementary school in then Czechoslovakia. So did my mother. But for my fanatical father the spa was always the German, Karlsbad." (4)

"For mine, too", Ute says, now again looking at her watch. "Their generation! We went there summers but I hardly remember it. Mother said he just had to take the waters once a year. Always in good health … yet he never came back from Russia. I think I was six the last time we saw Karlsbad … Karlovy Vary."

"You sound like me today, interviewing the returning POWs from Russia … who think they're being interrogated. That's my job … talking about the East. For the Amis. And espionage, sometimes finding a Russian deserter to send back to Russia as a spy for the Amis."

"Should you be telling me these things … top secret?"

"Oh, it is. I assure you. Top secret. But talking about it makes me feel free— and generous—just to say it out loud. Back then, back before the real war in the East began—peace pact with Russia or not—our invasion of Russia was around the corner. Everybody knew it. Russian speakers were needed. So since I already spoke Czech they sent me to a top secret language school in Oberammergau for Russian studies. Nearly the same language, they thought. Many many months, day and night. It was urgent. In the end I spoke like a Russian. So Gehlen and the Amis want me so I …"

"Helmut! Please stop! You have to stop … for now. My daughter. A babysitter. It's late. I have to go home. To Pullach."

"I'll drive you."

"No, no, I have my car. Uh, tomorrow if you like. Here?"

"Why not where I live? The Schloss Hotel. Just around the corner from here. Great view of the Isar Valley. Good restaurant. Tomorrow is strawberry day. Strawberries and whipped cream! Can't imagine I'm even saying such things. Back then we lived in mud and ice and ate rats in the cellars of Stalingrad. A realm apart from the rest … a filthy battleground that was our residence during the day. At night a kingdom belonging to the black rats and now it's bizarre that in the Schloss Hotel I request the smaller berries, tastier and tenderer than the big enticing ones. And I want my shirts ironed just so. Man is truly schizophrenic. Man can get used to anything … for survival."

## THEN THERE IS THE POWER OF WAR

I, Helmut W. Hartmann, Sudeten Deutscher, WWII, German *Abwehr* Military Intelligence in the East, flown out of Stalingrad in January 1943 and now an agent in top secret Gehlen Org, recognize the two real societies of this post-war Germany: on the one hand, the overwhelming majority of the defeated and only partially repentant society. And on the other, the occupiers, the Amis—not the French plural of friend— but the derogatory Amis-Americans. For we of the Gehlen Org know who really won the war: the Russians won the war. Not the Amis. The Amis occupied us but the Russians defeated us. That division still exists in some of our minds.

But in me something new churns. New visions take form. Ute's presence in my life has pointed out a new life direction. A new path. Something I've never before perceived. Never imagined. A feeling of potential fulfillment. Of totality. An almost unbearable sensation. After the everlastingly hopeless cold and *zapach voyny* of Stalingrad's cellars, I had never had an idea, not even the presentiment of the existence of such a feeling. Survival was my one and only life goal. Arrival in Munich as a resettled German from former Czechoslovakia: survival. War: survival. Rat-filled Stalingrad cellars: survival. Survival at all costs.

During the next nights we wake with our heads together on the same pillow, mouths close, her breath, my breath. Moments when hardly even the shadow of memories remain, the fleeting perception of the suspicion of something of the past, a vague remembrance of cold and rats flashing across my mind before dissolving again into her breath. I had always told my comrades that something of our pasts—of our collective pasts—resists seclusion and solitude. That something always remains. Somewhere in us. So on those dark gelid mornings they would ask me the Shadow as they called me, Herr *Schatten*, if any *Gespenster*—ghosts of the night—remained. They knew that my own personal *Gespenst* was only a black rat. One of the *Gespenster*-shadows running over me in the night.

And now some mornings on the balcony looking out over the Isar Valley toward Pullach she sings, deep, guttural, no hint of melody, drunk on love and hopeful sleep deprivation and we never think of sleep. No wasted time for us, yet we believe we have an eternity ahead. And on our pillow I don't see ghosts or black cellar rats. Ute's breath and its scents of forgotten perfumes fills the air around us like aromas of faraway dreams and holds the rat smells in my mind at bay. "Yes," I say, "love changes the world."

Over breakfast she asks about Gehlen. Hesitantly, she asks. No secrets from you, I reassure her, in one sentence purposefully breaking all the rules of my profession.

"What kind of a man is he?"

"Mysterious. But a child. Or a rat. Secretive by nature. Cynical. Believes in nothing but Reinhard Gehlen. At first his Foreign Armies of the East Intelligence and also the *Wehrmacht*

Intelligence in the East of which I was part tried to report the real truth to the Führer. The Leader didn't want negative truth. Unfazed, General Gehlen began working for himself. Mentally he began preparing to change sides. Was he a Nazi? I suppose he was. But already in 1942-43—like many top staff officers— he knew Germany had lost the war. Just a matter of time, he and the others believed."

"How did he know?"

"Ute, after that first winter we all knew that Germany wasn't ready for Russia. Germany would never be ready for Russia. We didn't even have the right clothing. How could we beat the cold? The Russians just fell back ... and waited. And they died for their land. Oh, how they died. By the millions. Civilians too. The SS men just killed anyone or everyone behind our lines. Did you hear about Zoya? No, how could you? A heroine in the Soviet Union. At eighteen she was a partisan behind our lines. When the SS hanged her, she said: 'There are two hundred million of us. You can't hang us all. They will avenge me. Stalin is with us. *Stalin s nami*. Stalin will come.' And even the SS knew they couldn't hang them all. You can't defeat people like that ... and the cold too."

"We had a few people like her right here in Munich. Sophie Scholl. Guillotined her! Not far from here."

"Good ... but not the same thing. *Komisch*, whatever we Germans speak of, we always come back to such stories. Sometimes I wonder why and how I got through and survived. And all in one piece. Oh, Ute, stay close to me."

Ute smiles her crooked smile that is becoming familiar. Her unique, unbounded and incomprehensible smile. One corner of her upper lip raised slightly higher than the other. And then the flick of the tip of her rose-colored tongue . The things Ute does! But how I love that tongue flick.

"Anyway, Gehlen began collecting data, saving maps, stashing away the true information about Eastern realities. At war's end, probably even earlier, he found his new sponsor: the United States. By 1946 his Gehlen Organization, Gehlen

Org, was set up in Pullach, across the Isar River from where we're sitting now and where you live. It's staffed by Nazis and infiltrators from the CIA who are more Nazi than the Nazis themselves."

"Helmut, you *are* in the wrong profession."

"Profession? It's a job. I was never a Nazi. I got into Gehlen's intelligence service thinking I was serving my country ... well, sort of my country. At least my people. But I never learned anything else. Only war! That's what my generation knows. War and more war. War and survival. We didn't learn other things ... Real life things."

"You definitely are in the wrong job."

"You're right but I've never known anything else. Still, I've got to get out of here."

"Good idea! That's something to talk about."

"Talk? They hear me talking like this, I'd not only be out of a job but really ... really out of everything. Did you know? —I mean how could you know in your film studio dedicated to what's fictitious, how could you know of a hit list of two hundred people right here in West Germany to be eliminated? Easy to get on that list. Deserters are the first. They kick me out of there, Ute, I might as well go back to Russia. You don't just resign and leave them. You don't get fired with a separation settlement either. Very powerful people down there in our Pullach. Evil people. And they made the CIA ... as much as the CIA made the Gehlen Org! Violence is doubly terrifying when it's in your own house. You become a prisoner in the prison you helped build. They emasculate you. They unman you. "

"Can you write, Helmut?"

"Write what? Situation reports? Russian troop displacements? Reserve strength? Troop morale in the Russian Third Infantry Division in Stalingrad? Leadership of Russia's Tenth Army? Oh, yes. Maybe even dispatches from the Eastern front. But write screen scripts? No way."

"Journalism, I mean. War stories. The cellars of Stalingrad. Eating rats. You have so much to say. Life experiences. Your stories make my scripts banal. Insipid and puerile. And all without that suffocating atmosphere of hyperbole we use there in Geiselgasteig."

"How? Where? And you don't even believe it's impossible to leave Pullach?"

"I believe you can. Leave, I mean. Others do. Even CIA agents leave and then write books. You can too. I've read about them."

I don't answer. But I know the rules. In peacetime I had just continued along the same old fucking rat-infested trajectory. Now love flowers and that changes everything. And so the weeds must die, I think poetically.

"I will introduce you to an old friend at the *Münchener Anzeiger*. Then we'll see. You have a life story to tell. Fiction too, if you like, based on your horrible life experiences. That kind of thing. For that you need magazines. I know a few. You might even go to Russia yourself instead of sending others ... see what's happening there now ten years later."

"Nasty, Ute! Nasty," I respond, for a moment my voice quivering. With ... with what? Indignation? Hopefully not pride. "But you're right and I'm wrong."

"Welcome to a new world, Helmut. The real world."

"Now I hope to get fired ...and not assassinated."

For all the wrong reasons I had thought there was nothing to be undone in me. Ute and love undid me for real in no time. A few words demolished me. Was I not a man of one piece? Of a morally rigid rectitude? I had few expressible convictions but admittedly an unspoken acceptance of things as they stood. There must have been in me a terror of the unforeseen disaster of Germany, a history which time could still turn around. Yet, before Stalingrad, I hadn't even perceived the dwindling sense of sublimity that our real history had promised.

## HANNICHKA

The first time I saw three-year old Hannah, I called her Hannichka. She laughed. So for me she has always been Hannichka. But at the time and under the top secret circumstances I couldn't see Hannichka when and as I wanted because she and Ute had to remain secret too. I knew that if our relationship were public Ute would be investigated; mysterious people would question her neighbors and enquire about her at the film studio. I wanted none of that for her. No, Ute must remain secret. So I couldn't just drop in after work— when there was an after-work. No, I had to drive my service car to Grünwald first. Park. Enter the Schloss Hotel. Have a drink. Wait a while until I knew the watchers were satisfied. Then change cars. In the hotel garage I have an old Opel from my father about which THEY probably knew anyway. And then I would drive back to Pullach. What kind of life is that? Inconsolable thought. Caught between the anvil and the hammer. The flimsy glories of the plane tree-lined streets lined by elegant the palais of my past were false images belied by the stench of the rat-infested cellars of Stalingrad. Confining and dangerous to stay in Gehlen Org; suicide to leave. Escape was a chimera, a hope to clutch at. For what was I except an old agent from the East, potentially, perhaps inherently a danger to the new masters.

One Sunday Hannichka and I leave her mother breakfasting on the Schloss Hotel balcony and set out by tram for downtown. Destination Blumenstrasse and the *Marionettentheater*. As the Strassenbahn winds its way along rubble-lined streets, where a kind of parallel life is going on in the cellars, Hannichka frowns and comments on the *fallen down houses*. Destroyed cities strike children. I t h o u g h t g o od she wasn't under one of the fallen down houses. At least by now they've transported much of the detritus of former

Munich to a growing hill on the old city airport from which you get a sweeping few of the razed city of the Wittelsbachs.

On the street Hannichka holds my hand. Handwritten words on walls read *Down With Hitler-Nieder mit Hitler*. Sophie Scholl messages. Church bells everywhere. Catholic Bavarians! The first thing they did after the bombs stopped falling was repair the church bells.

Hannichka pulls my hand and looks up at me: "*Glocken! Schöne Glocken.*"

I'm not Catholic. I'm not anything but I love the church bells … at a distance when they're soft and inviting. Not overhead where they sound like an artillery shell about to strike.

"We'll tell Mami about the pretty bells," she reminds me.

At Sendlingertorplatz a legless old man is sitting on a board. Hanging on his chest is a placard with the message:

*forget the color white*

*choose red the color of love.*

When I put two marks in the wooden plate, Hannichka asks what I bought. *Liebe*, I say. I bought love. She looks at me funny and holds my hand tight. A cool wind has come up. Rain is on the way.

*Fischer, Seine Frau* is playing in the puppet theater. The miniature opera house is packed with kids. The fisherman's wife wants it all: Mayorship, Presidency, Papacy.

"Oh," goes Hannichka when the witch flies across the boards to the far side of the stage to berate the fisherman. "*Ist sie gemein?*"

"Mean? I think so, yes," I say hesitantly. "Maybe a little cuckoo, too." Hannichka looks me in the eyes seriously, nods, then smiles and taps her temple with a forefinger.

All the kids are yelling comments to the puppets moving so lightly, barely touching the boards. Pure grace. Speaking Bavarian dialect. Hannichka understands. She would yell too the next time. Soon we would learn most of the repertoire. *Kasperl* and his adventures, *Hänsel und*

*Gretel*, operas for children. Hannichka cries and laughs and claps and I hug her and it's like hugging Ute.

Hannichka and Kasperl and the *Glockenspiel* convince me that Ute is right. This is real life. The war is over. I've got to get out of it.

## TEMPORARY RESOLUTION

"Ute, I have wartime friends in an Alpine village in Italy who still invite me there to the hidden valley called the Valtellina. They were saved by Italian Communists interceding in Moscow on their behalf and repatriated in 1946. We can leave it all behind us. I have some hidden funds. You have enough. We can live well there. You can write. I can try to write. Hannichka will live a normal life."

"Will you feel safe there? That's the question. For you, for me, for Hannah." "Yes, Ute. We can vanish, for now. Our Europe is huge. Its expanses. From Gibraltar to Greece, from Palermo to Berlin, from London to Sofia. The Alps and the Carpathians. The plains of Serbia, the steppes of Russia. The world's greatest cities are in our Europe. DeGaulle's Europe reaches to the Urals of Russia. Those unimaginable distances ... most marking a continent that our leaders have failed to delimit ... Napoleon wanted to. Then Hitler. Put it all under one roof. It never worked. We will be concealed somewhere in the immensity."

"Yes, my love, but huge in comparison to what? For a script I'm working on I had to study world atlases. I found that Europe is small. Actually, Helmut, we're not even a continent. It's clear and visible. You just have to look."

"Not a continent! Then what are we? What is the meaning of those words 'on the Continent'? You think we won't be safe down there, across the Alps ... inside the Alps in the Valtellina?"

"Oh, yes, we will be safe and secure. For now. Today, distances are still great. But tomorrow things will change. Wide highways and fast trains and cheap airplanes will change everything. And other Napoleons and other Hitlers and DeGaulles will come along and try to get us all under one tent. They're already talking about a union. Borders eliminated. One currency. Then you'll see how tiny this tip of the Euro-Asian peninsula called Europe really is. And Helmut, who really cares about us Europeans? Oh, we're quaint all right, our many incomprehensible languages and folksy ways and the taint, just a breath of danger attached. Foreign tourists love this bunch of once rich and divided countries with no voice in the real world. You think the so-called Cold War has anything to do with Europe? Europe is just the battleground, as usual. Oh, yes, it's a question of power, you know better than I. But it's not a question of Europe. Europe is war territory. A war zone. For the war between the Amis and the Russkies."

"Then no one will even think of us hidden away in those southern Alps. As if we never existed."

# PART THREE: OPERATION NIKU

I met Ramon on a bright October morning at the hour I like to watch the changing colors of the mountains. I was standing near what people in this Alpine village call the 'holy place', a spot marked by a red and blue ribbon fixed on a low stone wall running along the edge of the road on the hill above our house down in the village center.

Quiet reigned on the hill overlooking the valley called the Valtellina. I'd been observing a man strolling up the road toward me. I had glimpsed him a couple of times entering a house two doors down from our home on Via Piazza. This morning, now at some ten meters distance he grins at me as if I were an old friend and says *buon giorno* in a crisp yet somehow lazy Latin manner ... so different from the speech of the serious mountain people of Montagna, a people whose seeming completeness in their insouciance and their isolation from the rest of Italy is still inexplicable to Ute and me.

After an exchange of greetings, he speaks in such rapid Italian that I understand only that he'd seen me and *la bambina* walking up our street. "Oh, pardon! *Che lingua parla*?" he asks, leaning toward me and speaking louder than usual as people do to foreigners. "*Inglese* ... English?"

When I begin in my slow school English, he hears my accent and guesses correctly: "*Deutsch*!".

His name is Ramon. Ramon Dumitru speaks excellent German ... but he's not German either. So that I wonder how it happens that this non-German is living in this small Alpine village and how it happens that he speaks German so well. Ramon is about my age, and from his surname, Dumitru, he can only be Romanian. He's of average height with longish light brown hair and blue eyes making him look Scandinavian. A handsome man and apparently a man of some means, he lives with a good-looking Italian woman, not a native of the Valtellina either.

Now I'd known Romanians in my *Abwehr* Intelligence unit in Russia and there were Romanians in the Gehlen Org in Munich-Pullach … from which I am fleeing, so having him as a neighbor in tiny Montagna is, to say the least, alarming: like policemen, intelligence people don't believe in coincidences. And mysterious Ramon, man of several languages and considerable experience, is my neighbor!

So as we talk about where we come from it becomes clear from his allusions that Ramon too has lived in Munich and is connected with the Gehlen Org, a realization that makes me uncertain whether I should avoid him or gain his confidence and friendship.

From where Ramon and I are chatting, down in the valley the River Adda appears narrow, speckled with rocks jutting upward out of shadowed swirling, blue-silver-white waters. Although it resembles Munich's beloved Isar, I've come to dislike the Adda despite the river's attempts at mystery to overcome the reality of its brevity and the feebleness of its fluvial character. As it fights its way through the city of Sondrio below us the river appears uneasy in its confinement in the narrows between steep cliffs on the one side and solid rocky banks on the other. And uncannily it transmits its uneasiness to me. After issuing friskily from the Alps high above Stelvio Pass as if in search of freedom and after brashly cutting its way through the valley, farther to the west the Adda becomes navigable, stooping to offer cheap tourist jaunts, before, humiliatingly subdued, its waters fall meekly into Lake Como.

I dislike the River Adda because it resembles the Europe in defeat that shows in European faces. The defeated Europe I am fleeing from.

Ute, three-year old Hannichka and I left Munich in late September in this event-filled year of 1955. And even though the war ended ten years ago, the sensation of defeat still infects the nature of Europeans: so many historical events are taking place in the world this year that most people feel small and fearfully alone. After the conflagration of world war, the countless millions of dead and suffering and ubiquitous destruction, there are still millions of lonely and uprooted people wandering around Europe. The whole universe it seems was displaced by the war. Like the day I met Ute in the Gastätte in Munich-Grünwald, she'd still retained a fragment of her inherent aloneness even though she had her small daughter, Hannah, the generation of the future. And since the cellars of Stalingrad, aloneness was my very nature, too. I was the personification of aloneness.

Now today in Alpine Italy where everything is different we are again displaced, yet our togetherness is our defense against the pandemic malaise of loneliness. In that sense at least our separate lonelinesses are over and done with. Moreover, the presence of Ute's daughter simplifies such matters also for us; for Hannah is three-year old happy that we are all together ... and I believe because she now has a father. Actually, the only person she misses from Munich is her faithful baby-sitter-friend; she still wonders why Gudrun didn't come with us.

Ute and I had each arranged our personal affairs in such a way that we could simply drive away from Munich into the night: Ute became a freelancer for the film studio; while I—despite my qualms because of the nature of my work in top secret intelligence from which separation is rare—had dared resign with a mere registered letter mailed just before our departure ... actually the kind of rupture you prefer in life. Still, a registered letter bears heavy. It marks an end.

We traveled in Ute's roomy Opel, the car crammed with our stuff and skis on the roof. We passed through western Austria, into Switzerland, southwards past St. Moritz and the four-thousand-meter-high Piz Bernina, its peak a peculiar bluish red in a spectacular dawn sun. We entered Italy's Valtellina at the town of Tirana before turning west to our new home in the Alpine valley. On the map the valley called Valtellina appears as a long appendage to the belly of Alpine Switzerland, a long and narrow valley delimited in the south by the Orobic Mountains—beyond which lies classic Italy—and the Rhaetian Alps in the north, on the flanks of which lies the village of Montagna hanging over the city of Sondrio.

Now, only a month later, Ramon steps unwelcomed into my life. A symptom, a signal and reminder of the severe and brutal rules of the life from which I am separating. So Ramon is often on my mind. What to do is the question. Though I'm not exactly on the run, I don't want my presence here advertised either. Discreteness is the rule. And except for Ramon, my new life is a discreet life.

Sometimes I get up early mornings in order to see the unblemished whiteness of the light the sun casts on the mountain tops surrounding us, gradually eroding the resistance of the mountains to the loss of their pristine blue of the first dawn. That's the moment when I believe that the dawn's clarity might complete the healing of my Stalingrad wounds. For colors in the Alps are different. Stronger in their brilliance. And early morning is the time when any change might magically materialize. The time when the sun of the Valtellina begins its daily battle against the silence of life that to us newcomers seems to withhold more than it shows. A people harboring invisible lives. Montagna is also like the silence of a life not yet lived that you can feel during cool moonlit nights. In the Alps, the blue of morning is an uncanny moment for me personally. The moment when if you listen to the air and follow the colors you can come to believe the ancient legend that all things lost can be found again on the other side of the moon.

It is in the blue of those mornings when the purity of the valley below stares back at you the highflying observer that I feel most strongly that this is the time when Ute, Hannah and I have the chance to cut out new directions in the enduring post-war: just our being here in these chaste sparkling mountains offers us a new life. A life so different from our lives in Munich that I believe we will eventually succeed in shedding the look of defeat concealed underneath the superficial gaiety marking European faces of our times. The sham that marked my life before Ute. So I put my hopes in a life among a people in whose vocabulary words like Iron Curtain and Cold War will one day no longer exist.

Ramon and I meet often on the hill at the 'holy site', the name by which he said the priest at the Chiesa di San Giorgio and now most villagers call the place on the wall where we're talking. Sacred because it was here that a young Russian painter from Paris performed a miracle: he tied the shoelaces of the ragged village idiot who'd never before spoken and who from that moment began speaking perfect Italian. Right here. At our meeting place.

"A Russian? Here in Montagna? Pretty odd." "Odder than you and me being here? Two spies!"

"Ramon, you're a spy. I'm not. At least not anymore." "Smotri, Helmut! The whole fucking world is upside down. " "Very true! But I'm not a spy. You are!"

"Anyway, there was this kid everyone called the village idiot because he couldn't speak. And because he was dirty and dressed in rags. So one day this Russian guy is sitting here on the wall when the idiot walks by, his untied shoelaces flapping. The Russian gets him to sit down and tries to teach him to tie his shoelaces. The Russian finally ties them himself and the kid starts talking, BUT, the idiot doesn't want to learn to tie his shoelaces. He wants the Russian to do it. So the Russian does, every day, every day the ritual, and they become pals. Then the priest pronounces it a miracle and calls this spot sacred. He's still waiting for recognition of the miracle from the Vatican."

"So what happened to the Russian and the idiot? Where'd they go?"

"No idea! There was some car accident involving the idiot, so maybe the Russian took him back to Paris."

Or, on some afternoons, we meet in Grigione's bookstore just across the road from our observation point. The bookstore is more a meeting place than a commercial activity of which in Montagna there are only the caffé and a tiny, unattractive trattoria. The store interests me in particular because the proprietor too had lived in Munich for twenty years and had returned to his home to open his dream bookstore … not so much to sell books, Grigione says, as to collect them and live among them.

Still, I ask myself if Grigione the Collector's presence here, all his books and German newspapers, are coincidence, too. Or am I paranoid?

Ramon is a different story. It becomes clear that he's a very ambitious man—a typical Romanian characteristic he himself once said. The sky is the only limit for him. And he is prepared to risk everything to get there. Now I think he just wants to become an influential rich American… as if he were no longer accountable to his former self. For that reason, his apparent patience with life in this village is out of character. He's always waiting. Waiting and waiting. So I wonder for what? And in any case, why here?

The day at the holy site I mentioned Stalingrad, he reacted in a curious manner to my admission of my *Abwehr* background and that I was in the cellars of Stalingrad before the surrender of the German Sixth Army. In his soft, almost sensuous manner he revealed that like many of the 580,000 Romanian soldiers in Russia he too had been in Hitler's army at Stalingrad, but that unlike the hell it had been for me, it was a wonderful time for him: he'd been assigned to General Reinhard Gehlen's *Fremde Heere Ost*, FHO (Foreign Armies East) a German parallel intelligence organization. He never ate horse brains broth or rat steaks.

For myriad reasons—my *Abwehr* background, my Gehlen link, my coming here from Munich and my presence in Montagna—Ramon believes I am still linked to Gehlen. For he too is hiding … from something or someone. And in his mind so am I.

# UTE FRIEDRICH HARTMANN

Sometimes Ute falls into an impenetrable silence, a sense of stillness within her, a sort of total lifelessness in which she doesn't speak at all. In such moments she doesn't want to be talked to by others whose words meet a silent stone wall … as if spoken in some Andean dialect. Then, abruptly, the moment passes and she starts again in her usual reflective manner.

One day when I asked her what it was like in the homeland during the last days of the war she emerged from such a silence as if she'd been thinking precisely about that period.

"After the bombings, I felt … I felt unraveled. Totally. So at the end the thing I most wanted was silence, the silence of other unraveled people like me." She pauses, reflects and says mysteriously: "I aspired to the presence of those words that are never spoken."

"Which words? Which words do you mean? And was your American conqueror -friend also unraveled?" I asked anyway … as I always do when the film of separation sheds her eyes and I feel a certain jealousy of exclusion from the her of those times.

"Oh yes, he was unraveled. And how! But he was just too, too … oh, how can I say it? Too innocent. Too American. Too young … both in years and experience. He didn't know what war was. He'd never known bombs falling. He didn't understand things like we do. He was searching, I suppose. He was good and decent… but too young in every way. Young like I imagine most Americans are. And he had no real center. No roots holding him in place like we once did. I liked him a lot but I would never have married him and gone to America with him. What would I, a European to my quick, do there? Submit to another? No, I wasn't ready to abandon my own self. I was pregnant but I sent him away so I could have Hannah alone.

"But what about love and romance and all that in your life. Didn't you miss it?"

"Oh, yes, of course. But love? I have always needed love. But I came to realize that I can love only a man who still wants to change the world. Who wants to make things better ... and who doesn't expect my submission. Maybe I too am just a fragment. Maybe we all are. But I want control of the fragment that is me."

"So what about me? You show that you love me ... though I don't want to do anything to change the world."

"I think you do. You just don't know yourself ... not yet. The world has had its way with you ... until recently. Now you've said: *genug*! Enough! You showed you are one of those who want to go beyond. (Go *jenseits*, she said, meaning out there  into unexplored territory.) Some women don't like that. It seems too abstract. I do though. And you changed all our worlds when you broke through and brought the three of us here to this village, to this valley where things are quiet ... but mysteriously, maybe secretively, alive."

"I was just running. But then, Ute, it was the right thing to do."

"The right thing to do, the right thing to do! Of course it was. Helmut, I recognized you when I first saw you. When you came to my table that day in Grünwald carrying two glasses of beer. That look in your eyes of the man constantly reviewing his own life. *Ecce homo*, I thought. And then, Helmut, your father-daughter relationship with Hannah cemented also our relationship."

Ute was right. I wanted to be together with her and loving her I also wanted Hannicka to be my daughter. So we married and I adopted Hannah. And we became the Hartmanns ... in Germany. But in Italy, Ute retains her name: Friedrich. She likes that. But her daughter is Hannah Hartmann. I like *that*. Complex laws indeed!

This morning, again, after a long silence at her desk during which she hadn't moved even a hand, Ute said: "To think that we're only a day's drive from our old home but that our new home in the Valtellina is itself a world apart. Melancholy. Silent. Maybe lonesome. Officially, a *depressed area*. And—just imagine, this isolated valley hasn't known real war for centuries. Only Mussolini's defeated Fascists wanted to make a new country here. But that was just a dream."

"Hmm!" I muttered and waited. There was more to come. Extraordinary the duality in that woman!

"So why do I suspect that a feeling of hopelessness lies underneath these people's veneer of joy and exuberance? Helmut, I sense in them the spirit of a conquered people. Like us in that. People here are separate, yes. But they're not a race, nor a nation. Yet they are at least a people. But then maybe all Italians—also those down south beyond the mountains—are like these people. They've been conquered so many times that ..."

"Yes, Ute, but they're still here. Italy absorbed the conquerors. Phoenicians and Arabs, Swiss, Germans, Austrians, Normans and Spanish. Some conquered and victimized peoples do that. Over time the victims prove to be stronger than the victimizers and suck the essence of the conquerors ... and their features too. Like the Norman blood running through the veins of those blond and blue-eyed Sicilians I read about? And those of the dark skins of their Arab conquerors."

"What a mishmash our Europe is! Because the conquered also take on some of the characteristics of the conquerors. Some of them anyway. Like Italian guest workers in Germany, the *Gastarbeiter* ... they seem arrogant and superior but submissive at the same time."

"Not the Russians though. Maybe they're the exceptions. Not the ones I encountered anyway. They are a people, a nation and even nearly a race. *Russki Narod*. The Russian people. How many times I heard it. *Russki Narod*. The invaders arrive and they conquer only scorched earth. No sustenance for invaders there. *Pustaya Territoriya*. No invaders can undo them … not like the occupiers have undone us. Why we're even becoming more like them, the charmless but powerful occupiers. For a while the Russians were conquered and slaughtered, but they never surrendered. They never surrendered anything of themselves to us Germans. Nothing. Only *pobeda* counted. Victory. There were some traitors, of course. There are always some weak of spirit. And then, remember, even Gehlen himself was a traitor."

"Helmut, you've never told me how it really was in Stalingrad. You don't like to talk about it. But I need to know. How can I know you if I don't know this about you?"

"Stalingrad. Ute, I talk about it with myself non-stop. Stalingrad. I see images. Random images. Flashes. Fragments. Forty below zero, denim uniforms. A slice or two of bread per day. Some soldiers used their entrenching tools to crack the skulls of frozen horses to make a broth from the boiled brains. Then, the war. How can you operate a submachine gun when your hands are completely numb? How can you take shelter from the cold anywhere when every building is in shambles? Wouldn't a fire attract too much attention from the enemy? The snipers. Theirs and ours. A terrible kind of war. You're eating frozen horses' brains, and the next second you're dead. If you take refuge in the sewers where everything is frozen Russian patrols find you … since no able-bodied German soldier would protect you down there. In those times Russian war prisoners were left to freeze and starve to death within open-air enclosures … after having been stripped of their *Valenki*-winter boots. Reports of cannibalism among them. Later on also among Germans within the Pocket of Stalingrad. But of the 90,000 Germans that surrendered in the end, most died of typhus in the POW Camps. Still, curiously, some of us in Stalingrad remained fatter than others. Then we discovered the ring of cannibals. My rat steak was likely a human steak. Oh, Ute! It's just too much to put into words. Better such words remain unspoken."

"Easy. Easy," Ute said softly. "But about conquerors and the conquered, we Germans are different! We too absorb our conquerors, but we become much like them. Not people here. Here, underneath, at their quick, people here in the mountains and valleys are resilient and resistant and complete. No one is like them ... except maybe your Russians. Still, in their sense of completeness they're careless. An indifferent kind of carelessness as to what is happening across the mountains to the south ... or now that I think about it also carelessness even about those secret armies lurking in Italy's hidden places that you talk about with Ramon."

"Oh, Ramon! Incomprehensible Ramon."

"I'll never trust him. And I can't understand your tolerance in his regard." "Maybe tolerance, Ute ... but little trust. I don't understand him. Therefore, my suspicion of who he really is. No trust in him whatsoever until I learn what his game is. And, Ute, I'll find out one way or another."

The month of October passed. Time seemed strange in those days. Clocks didn't go. Time fell off ... as if forgotten. Until one evening we went with Ramon and Giuliana to dinner in the neighboring mountain town of Teglio, where by chance my Communist friends live. Ramon said we had to taste the *pizzoccheri*, the pasta specialty of the area. Our first time! Hannah knew the word and called the town by its name in dialect, *Tei*, like the older kids in the kindergarten. Incredible how small kids can learn a foreign language so quickly; even if she had no idea what the word meant. She just parroted the others ... and soon the word fell into place.

Teglio is a very old town. Also a town of stone. Stone walls and streets where in the mysterious darkness of winding alleys and artistic arches the dark courtyards give off emptiness and loneliness ... even the negation of life. Where for long moments I hear only the sliding of my own feet on the stones. The smelly brown-red flames of the torches illuminating its ancient streets make you aware of the deepness of the dark mountain night. In the crisp air the bougainvillea hangs heavy, sad and colorless in the shadows. Their world of shadows is frightening. And I hold tighter Hannah's hand. I still have the curse of dark and cold cellars. The antediluvian silence of the timeless obscurity of Teglio's non-illuminated alleys recall the terror of late night ruins of Stalingrad streets where time had stopped. And I shiver inwardly.

We enter a sprawling cobbled piazza from which wider streets branch off. The little mountain town has suddenly become vibrant and alive with people and cars bringing loud diners from villages stretched across the flanks of the Rhaetian Alps. A fountain-like pond in the center is illuminated by low-hanging street lamps to exhibit groups of white and pink water lilies, uncanny flowers that emanate no scent at all. I look down at Hannah. She is frowning and says that the lilies look sleepy. *"Sie wollen schlafen"*. And after a hesitation: *"in questo chiasso."*

"They're sleepy ... in this noise," Ramon translates both languages automatically.

The restaurant is animated. Waiters rush back and forth, getting the pasta to their regulars first. I look around the room searching for the once familiar faces of my friends but uncertain and a bit forlorn that I would not recognize them after all the years. Then over the pizzoccheri we talk randomly about our new home, the mountains and the valleys while I peer about the space from one table to the next.

Ramon and I gradually drift back to the war. Both of us Stalingrad veterans. Both of us with links to German Intelligence and with Gehlen. In veiled terms we recall how each of us experienced it and how we remember it now, ten years later. My memories: horror. His: adventure and excitement. Yet somehow our memories overlap, perhaps because of our similar origins: I, from the ethnic German part of Czechoslovakia and he, from nearby Romania.

What interests me is how Ramon sees the war now. War in general. The thing is he's not anti-war at all. Yet he's so charming—probably deceptively so, because, I realize, I've never seen any signs of genuine kindness in him. Politeness, yes, But little real kindness. Little real warmth. Cold underneath his words. He seems to constantly suppress a wild ferocity toward the world … like the cruelty Romanian soldiers in Russia displayed toward the conquered. Although the war treated Ramon well, he still has a terrible hate in him. So he seems shocked when I blurt out my anti-war feelings.

He and I truly see the world with different eyes. While I speak of my attraction to the idea of the collective of the Russians and all that implies for post-war Europe, Ramon professes a total individualism. He thinks it is the war that made of him a complete and accomplished individual. And he has no illusions whatsoever about the collective, whether, as he says unambiguously, of the Stalin or of the Hitler stamp.

While I feel the ugliness and the horror, the uselessness of what we both experienced, Ramon sees it as a breakthrough for himself, the chance for a new understanding of life. Still, Ramon remains undefined for me … and unconfined in his ambitions. He has already grasped chance. *Carpe diem*, he says, is his motto. *"Enough of a life of blind abstractions. Enough of feelings of hanging suspended between the two worlds of the old, brutal pre-war and the new problematic post-war. There are three drives in man, Helmut: ambition, a great idea and inspiration. I choose the first. No more suspension for me; no more abstractions; only reality counts. Communism, capitalism, fascism—even freedom—are just chains. One individual. Here I am, complete and done. Enough submission. Enough of just letting happen whatever seems destined to happen. I am for me."*

He pronounces his vicious convictions in short phrases, in a low voice, in German, his Latin eyes gleaming, his facial features momentarily transfigured. Then he stops to translate to Giuliana who has sat silently, a permanent look of bewilderment on her face that she was hearing such talk here in Teglio. Heavy talk. Heavy like the pizzoccheri we are eating.

I start to object, then shrug and turn back to the too heavy pasta. You can't argue with ambition. Ute, who usually listens to such talk in silence, opens her mouth to protest but then she too remains silent. Her silence rings like a message to me: 'Don't ever trust that man.' Meanwhile, Hannichka has dropped off to sleep, her head in my lap and I stroke her hair absent-mindedly.

"Ramon," I say to change the subject, "I've wanted to ask you about your travels. One day you're here, the next day you're gone … and you're gone for some time. Giuliana gets lonely, you know." We've gotten to know Giuliana during his absences. And she loves Hannah and Hannah, her, which has endeared her to us.

"My parents in Romania are old. I have to take care of them. I go to visit when I can, see to what has to be done … and I put things in order," he says is his ambiguous manner.

"So why not take Giuliana with you?" Ute asks naively. She doesn't suspect that his visits to Romania—if he goes only there and not also Munich-Pullach—are not family visits at all.

"Oh, it would be boring for her," Ramon begins, his light eyes turning steely as if unseeing while his voice remains low and surprisingly melancholy. "And then Romania is so complex … now."

I've never believed for a minute that an ambitious man like Ramon spends all that time taking care of his parents … who anyway seem well off … now. I suspect his work has to do with American and Gehlen relations with Romanian Communists.

"Oh, Gehlen and CIA people too know about my friends in the Romanian Communist Party," he says in German. "They approve of it. Want me to go ahead with it. They're curious about my predictions of a brilliant future for an ambitious guy I know pretty well, named Nicolae Ceausescu." (5)

He had told me that the Romanian Leader, Gheorghiu-Dei, was not well. Many changes will happen in Romania when he dies. And I believe the new Romania to come is part of Ramon's job: courting Ceausescu, who just last year was named to  the Politburo. Now for whom would Ramon do such tasks? For Gehlen of course. And for Gehlen's bosses, the Amis. U.S. policy is to drive a cleft in the new Warsaw Pact of Communist East Europe. And Ramon is one of their doubles. A double agent.

Ramon had also told me that Romanian Communists are divided between the "home Communists" in contrast to the "Muscovites" loyal to the Moscow hard line. Ceausescu would become a popular man in the West—but a maverick in the East because of his "opposition" to Moscow. "Nicky"—as Ramon sometimes calls him— believes Romania should be a world power.

Ambitious Ramon sees himself on a future Ceausescu team. A Trojan Horse in Communist Romania. Ceausescu like Ramon wants to be part of the West. Ramon is pissed that Westerners don't even know that Romanian is a Romance language … thinking it's Slavic. Spoken Romanian sounds Italian though the grammar is different, and words have different meanings. He likes the example of going to Roma … or Bucharesti. Italian: *Oggi vado a Roma*. Romanian: *Astazi plec la Bucaresti*. He has me repeat it over and over until I hear clearly the Latin language in the phrase.

"Romanian is a Romance language, Like Spanish and Portuguese. Like Italian itself," he adds. "And we belong in the West."

"Speaking Italian came to me over night," he once told me, "as it happens to most Romanians living in Italy. Shows how close our languages are. Crazy, when you think about it. But after all we do belong to the West. Niku thinks the same. He wants to head the Non-Aligned Movement.

Wants Romania—*his* Romania—to be more than a satellite of the Soviet Union."

One day from my window I saw three men get out of a black suv parked in front of Ramon's house. So I waited. Sure enough, when they came back out, they were four: Ramon, elegantly dressed from head to toe in black, did not look happy. He kept looking over his shoulder and saying something to Giuliana standing in the doorway. From my front steps I waved. He only blinked in recognition.

Spontaneously I thought: Gehlen people.

Ramon returned three days later. That same afternoon we met at the holy site. And point blank I asked him where he'd been. Almost carelessly, he sat down on the wall just next to the red and blue ribbon marking the sacred spot.

And he looked up at me and said: "I was in Pullach." Some time passed. Then I said: "So?"

"So, there were also Amis present," he said and grinned evilly. "And now I'm top priority."

"Top priority? What does that mean?"

"Before—I learned—they'd just scanned my reports and filed away my stuff about the man in Bucharesti— Nicolae Ceausescu,[6] the man I've mentioned to you. Now they've decided to make a big investment in him. And I'm a double."

"Why that? Why him? And what kind of investment?"

"Even though my previous reports were ignored, big changes are coming. Nicky—Niku as they prefer to call him—has become official. 'Operation Niku they call it'. And I am the point man in the field ... for a while at least. I suspect only for as long as they need me."

"So you'll be leaving us and Montagna?" "Not for now. I'm more secret here." "Like me, eh?"

"They didn't even mention you!"

Still, his story rings outrageously crazy. Oh, the eternal femaleness of intelligence agencies: always searching for the grand project, the great operation, the person to change the course of history ... like the other half of their souls. And they expect to find love there ... for their efforts. On the other hand they are infected with the eternal duplicity of maleness: war and blood ... and the same search for love. Yet for their reasons, whatever they are, they've let me go. I'm free. But they've found a double! A feather in their caps.

So today I feel good and secure in these mountains hanging over the Valtellina. We will stay here in this land surrounded by the Alps. Our sanctuary. And refuge. Where the greatest noise—Hannichka's *chiasso*—are the infernal bells of the Church of San Giorgio. So that I've come to feel that those turbulent bells mark the regular passing of time, the regular manner in which we want time to pass. Regularly passing time is emblematic of the security fragile humans search for—and for Ute and me a reminder of our reality ... and at the same time of who we are. They measure and synchronize our lives with the passing of time, here so uniform and unvarying.

If it's true as Dostoevsky said that time itself is both illusory and eternal, I too am admittedly still in search of a perfect time. And perhaps San Giorgio's bells moderate time's mystery by lying to us that time is even, regular and always the same. Sometimes I am soothed by the church bells insisting on that constancy. Other times I am disturbed by time's very passing— each clang marking another fragment of the time of our unreal uprooted lives—after all only a one day's drive from home.

## PART FOUR: THE POWER OF WOMAN

On their return home the Hartmanns had no illusions that they would find the same post-war Munich they had fled from two decades earlier. Nonetheless they were astonished to find what seemed another city altogether. But then they realized that they *had* been gone twenty event-filled years. Those years had transformed not only the visible city they had known but had also erased that unseen but perceived air of defeat and prevailing gloom of resignation on the faces of München's people.

During their absence—their exile, Helmut called it— the piles of ruins and skeletons of bomb-demolished buildings of the devastatingly foreign city of then too had disappeared. Now, the palaces and great buildings—in regal Munich called *palast* and *palais*—had been recreated in all their magnificence … precisely as they were before the war. Yet the old men on their fourth mass of beer in the big hall of the Hofbräuhaus on a Saturday morning swore that this was not the real Munich either, the Munich of when Mensch was Mensch and a mass of beer was a full liter, and—back in the good old times—when even the beer was sweeter.

None of the three had dreamed of a return to Grünwald and Pullach … least of all Hannah, who didn't remember where they had lived before Italy. Only from hearsay was she even German. For Helmut and Ute too that former life was over and done with. Again in their homeland they were beginning everything anew. And as Ute noted, Helmut acted as if he'd never had an enemy in the world. Yet he too, the repeat returnee, had his black memories to deal with. His private black holes. Remembrances of the bad times still haunted him. Remembrances of totalitarianism in his world and of what for a time had seemed the absolute evil, the embers of which he felt smoldering in his depths. The same combination of the same circumstances had hindered his return for the two long yet short decades in Italy.

He said he didn't desert his home country as he thought he should have. On the contrary. He'd felt he was the abandoned one. He'd thought he could never forgive his homeland for its betrayal and even less than others could he forgive it its evil. Unfeeling evils in the homeland and in the unspoken words of the contagion it emitted spreading across the Atlantic … only a pond it turns out separating them one from the other. Only an easily traversable pond. One evil had produced another.

For the first ten years abroad he'd been vocally bitter. His bitterness had since matured like smoldering embers to combat level. Society was changing but far from enough. No penance had been done … and far too little repentance. He was rebelling against that evil … still circulating as it had before his exile, stubbornly refusing to eliminate itself and become extinct. And today, as through a veil darkly, he repeated to Ute, he could see his own rebellion swirling and whorling in the Teutonic air.

He and his whole family were starting over. And they were fortunate, Helmut recognized. They were free of economic restrictions: they could choose any part of the city they fancied to live in … space was the foremost requirement. Helmut Hartmann was now an affirmed journalist; Ute Friedrich, a screen writer. And Hannah, a twenty-three-year-old beauty, newly graduated from Milan University who wanted to live her own life, continue with her painting and above all learn what her Germanness really was and what it meant to be a German today. Were all Germans still either devils or rehabilitated angels?

The Hartmanns settled in a big duplex penthouse on the corner of Teng- and Elisabeth Strasse in the heart of the academic, cultural district of Schwabing: Hannah upstairs with a light-filled studio and her privacy; Ute and Helmut downstairs where they too had separate studios.

Now, Helmut thought, after my youth in Sudetenland in Czechoslovakia, after dislocation and resettlement in Germany, after Stalingrad and Gehlen Org in Pullach and after the Valtellina in Italy, I finally have a set location. And the keys to it. It's mine. It's ours. So now the rest is up to me. And perhaps with help from fate or the omnipresent *sudba,* the sound of which he loved in Russian. I'm not done in … nor am I done yet. I'm only now starting out in real life. A beginner. A *pivello*, as Hannah said in Italian of herself.


## MUNICH


The city. Trying to get a handle on the city he again walked it. From palais to palais, from bridge to bridge along the banks of the Isar. The new luxury apartments in Bogenhausen replacing the rundown post-war *plattenbau* blocks. Not only the physical city was different. Helmut, man of several countries, was a new man.

The city. Helmut felt like a transplant, a *Zugereister*, as Müncheners called new arrivals. He saw things today in a different light. People too were different. They'd forgotten the bombs that destroyed their city. He'd been sort of Czech, Czech-German, German, Münchener, sort of Italian. Now he walked the city he loved in search of his own Germanness. He saw Hitler's places clearer than before. He saw the beer gardens. The Oktoberfest. But avoided the beer cellars that real Germans loved. He rode out to the airport. Still world travelers, these Germans. Stared at lines of people at the racetrack placing their bets. Müncheners all? He walked to Nymphenburg Palace to see the Amalienburg, the rococo hunting lodge in the palace park. Jammed with foreign tourists. Took the tram back home.

The city. September mornings seemed cooler than before their life in Italy. Only occasionally sunny. The usual dark clouds hung forever in ambush. Clouds that might unexpectedly part and a rare deep blue sky would peep out and sunshine crash down onto their corner of Earth and turn the

Isar waters to silver. The constant rain and sudden sun and showers were like everything else; life was so unpredictably different from the southern Alps of his last twenty years.

Real Munich was not the city Helmut had conjured up in his imagination while in exile. Today he didn't know what to make of the city he had loved in that crazy-terrible post-war way. No more than he had known what to make of the real Italy, the Italy down there beyond the pre-Alps to the south of their Valtellina home. His contact with "real Italy"—as he called it—was chiefly Milano when they visited Hannah while she studied there. But Munich was anyway still part of him. And he'd once been part of it: he'd been at the parades celebrating its 800$^{th}$ anniversary and parades marking the day the one millionth Münchener was born; he'd followed the reconstruction of the war-ravaged Bavarian State Opera House. Now it was all reality. The Königsplatz was again like before the war.

Wherever he had been in the East or later in the Alps or Milan, it seemed his way had always led back to *föhn*-blown Munich—protective eye shades against that warm southern wind from the Alps, air purifiers and endless anti-allergic medications notwithstanding.

Milan-Milano had reminded him of his imaginary Munich, the trams winding their way over narrow cobblestoned streets through both cities, both their cathedrals heavily damaged by Ami bombs. Or maybe it was only their same initial M. And the night train of Wagons Lits running between the two cities. In any case, in reality they did not seem so different one from the other as he had once imagined. On one of the dark mornings that Helmut thought of as symbolic of Munich, they were sitting near the big window in Ute's studio where from the fourth-floor lookout he was watching Hannah rush down the wide sidewalk of Tengstraase in her firm, self-confident gait.

"Ute," he said, his eyes following Hannah's familiar figure nearing the corner, "I can hardly believe this young lady and university graduate is the three-year old I used to take to the Puppet Theater. Time got away from us. Now that we're back home again the twenty years in Italy seem to have hardly happened. Just another memory ... of a place we used to know."

He frowned at his own words, cleared his throat and lit a cigarette, the snap shut of his Zippo lighter ringing louder than usual as if it too doubted the count: "Twenty years, Ute! Twenty! And our child is an adult."

"That's the way time is, Helmut. It's never even and regular as we like to think. It's our clocks and calendars that confuse us. And day and night ... and the seasons. It's our life, yes, but all its images still end up in scrapbooks ... with the rest of life."

"Right. But still, still ..." He lost his train of thought. Ute was so philosophic.

"Still what, my love?"

"Well, circumstances change so fast. Us, for example. While Hannah was growing up, you and I did so many things. Think of that a bit. And we just stayed on in an Italy that was never ours. Year after year, another decade, then another. We could have come back home years ago ... but didn't. Why didn't we?"

"Well, there were Hannah's schools and her friends and then just a way of life ... we got used to it."

"But you and I? We never really amalgamated. We lived in Italy ... even though the Valtellina didn't really seem like Italy. We adapted. We know our way around there; we know Italy but we remained who we were: Germans."

"But also Europeans!" Ute added. "Makes you wonder!"

"What do you mean? Wonder what?"

"Wonder about being also Europeans. Seems like many people are perplexed about what it means ... to be a European, I mean. Every day I ask myself if I even want to be one any longer."

"Still, some people do want to change things around. The whole system, I mean. Nazis destroyed our generation and now they're coming back to power. And not only here. Crazy, no!"

"New Europe is at the city gates!"


## REVOLUTIONARIES OR TERRORISTS?


From Italy, Helmut Harmann had written about the Red Brigades. His own newspaper had  called the anti-capitalist *Rote Brigaden* "terrorists". But not Helmut Hartmann. For him they were a "resistance movement". Revolutionaries. Like in Russia. Like in France. In wartime Italy too. Resistance was resistance to aggression. Resistance against enemy invaders. Mad Nazis considered them terrorists to be punished, again and again for such thoughts.

While rumors circulated about assistance from the Palestinian PLO and from Communist East Europe and while millions of Italians lent the Red Brigades their moral support, his Romanian friend, Ramon now a big wheel in Ceausescu's socialist government in Bucharest—who still came for short stays in Montagna—swore that no one in East Europe would support "Red Brigade terrorists." Especially not since the Italian Communist Party too had disowned them. Deserted by the official left, the exteme left *Brigate Rosse* ended up alone.

In those post-1968 years, Helmut, writing from Alpine Italy, had concentrated on the Red Brigades. Now, back in Munich, he zeroed in on their cousins in Germany, the Red Army Faction, or RAF. He knew their history well. Both revolutionary underground organizations were born between 1968 and 1970, part of the backlash to the US war in Vietnam, RAF however chiefly because of the return of so many Nazis to positions of power in West Germany. After his return to Munich in 1975, Helmut also traveled around Germany, frequently to Italy, and occasionally to Paris to speak with Italian left-wing revolutionaries who after the crackdown were granted asylum in France.

Had he himself not fled from Germany to Italy in the first place because of the widespread Nazi presence in power in Germany, especially in Gehlen's organization where he worked? He knew first-hand what was happening in Germany. But then came the disillusionment at the CIA-Gladio-Fascist power in his country of exile. His journalism by its nature was of the investigative type: his goal, he told Ute, was to uncover the real power centers in new Europe: political power always infiltrated opposition groups like the Red Brigades, like RAF. Political power turned them and used them against themselves … and the nation. History shows it, he thought: the worst enemy of revolutionaries is within themselves.

He loved the quote from a letter Gudrun Ensslin—co-founder and the intellectual brain of RAF—wrote to her companion, Andreas Baader: *"... what's been missing in the European fight for socialism over the last 100 years is the element of 'madness.'"*


## HELMUT SEIFERT HARTMANN


Winter. The low December sky, dark and dreary. From his window he observed the winter east wind blowing from Elisabethstrasse. Small trees near the corner bent nearly to the pavement under the force, then magically rose again straight up during a lull. Visibly cold down there on Tengstrasse where a man wearing a winter coat and a Russian Ushanka hat pulled down over his ears leaned forward into the wind in a mighty struggle for supremacy. Had he too been in Stalingrad? The man was carrying two bottles of milk, one under his arm. Suddenly Helmut knocked on the window and shouted:

'Careful, the bottle's slipping.' It did. *Kaklop kaplash* on the sidewalk. A pond of milk and glass surrounded the lone man like a stranger in a strange land looking in consternation at the spreading white mess as Helmut's philosopher friend in the Stalingrad cellar did when his tin filled with horse-brain broth had slipped from his cold numbed hands and spilled; finally the man on Tengstrasse just shrugged and looking over his shoulder and wiping at the white on his shoes hurried on hoping no one had noticed.

That day Helmut closed the door to his office-study in order to be alone with his ruminations. Again, as often of late, he recited to himself the only words he recalled of a poem by Jaroslav Seifert, the Czech poet his father had loved and even named his own son after him. *Sometimes we are tied down by memories/ and there are no scissors that could cut/through those tough threads/ or ropes.*

Now what did the poet have in mind when he added those two last words: 'or ropes'? Why ropes? Black Nazi ropes? Ropes of habit? Of ingrained beliefs? Of Self? Of veils through which to see only darkly? Or ropes of total insulation … stopped up with fingers in my ears? Or ropes to hang oneself? Things at times seemed so … so amorphous, so without any form or structure at all. Inchoate objects about to become something.

In any case, after the cold cellars of Stalingrad, Helmut Seifert Hartmann came to love in a special way the poet's words: *I believe that seeking beautiful words is better than killing and murdering.* And he saw himself as in a portrait, the portrait of  a man who felt fortunate simply because he'd never killed anyone in the war … never even shot the pistol which was just part of his *Abwehr* uniform.

With mounting dissatisfaction he turned away from the window and remembered there had been times when he admitted that he just didn't give a fuck if they lost the fucking war. As a matter of fact, he'd hoped they did. But then, as he had in Stalingrad, he remembered fondly his father's telling him again and again that in the 1920s his poet namesake was enthusiastic about the Russian Revolution and had joined the Communist Party. And secretly Helmut Seifert Hartmann regretted that he had never had such a chance. An unhappy thought that never abandoned him. One of those hidden desires, words never revealed, words never spoken. For most certainly he *had* hoped to jeopardize the interests of his times, in which he, fortunately, was seldom the right age—either too young or too old. Only right on time for a dark cold rat-infested basement in Stalingrad where you could die either of starvation and cold or a sniper's bullet.

From the start he had never intended being a mere newspaper reporter. He might speak of himself as a reporter, but he knew he had too heavy a load of experience to even think of just reporting. To hell with conciseness and synthesis. Above all, to hell with impartiality. Roaming around in his fervid mind there were  too many straightforward words that had to be spoken. Unambiguously. He'd written enough useless fact-filled reports for the Abwehr Intelligence to last him a lifetime. His post-war life was now over and gone too. Gone, yet still present. For in a sense it still existed. The shadow that remains from disappeared objects and times and persons. Their shadow was still present. Stupid lifetime. Stupid experience, his military service. And Gehlen. Especially Gehlen. Another time of which he never spoke. In particular not of the Gehlen time. A part of his life hidden away somewhere between his unconscious—if it existed—to which Freud referred. Hopeful monster of an idea! In his active memory at least Gehlen time was definable: the most evil part of his life experience! However that may be, he repeated, the sum of those experiences are mine alone. But one thing is clear, he thought, slapping one hand into the other: 'Stalingrad made me into what I am today. For good or for bad. At least that. So unlike his Romanian friend in Montagna, Ramon, who had described Stalingrad as wondrous adventure—after it was over. But the pure experience of Stalingrad, the nitty-gritty part, the rats and the cannibals, tough but life-determining experiences—no actual report writing from a cellar!—had left him exposed, transformed and transfigured. Converted to something, or to someone else. Never would he lose the memory of it. Oh, no! Never. He struggled to hold tight to that memory ... in all its nuances, in all its ramifications. Stalingrad was the long moment that changed him ... and its memories became his memories. His right. His possession. His obsession.

Yet, he told himself, he didn't think that his experience was exclusive to him. Selfish. Bourgeois individualism—a word he'd begun thinking of late. And had even used it once to Ute, inadvertently. He recalled how she had looked at him in a funny way.

*Komisch!* Still, in the end the mind gets its own way. *Bourgeois individualism,* he repeated to himself. Yet others did have a right to his thoughts about his experiences too.

The Buddhist part of him wanted to share his thoughts. To transcend the sorrow and evil of his personal experience. But not completely. Not totally. Not expressly so. Share it more simply, but also more complexly. Share a life experienced in a certain way. To accomplish that, he feared, he would have to dig deeper into himself ... to be able to explain it correctly to others. He too loved simple words, everyday words, as did Seifert the poet. He thought in terms of essence, in terms of the core of people and things ... even if of invented people and things even though still, still, still, inchoate and amorphous. But invented by himself. Ex-novo. From nothing to something. Words had to form inside him and emerge from him. Words. Most of which were still unspoken.

Above all, Helmut hoped for an eventual understanding of what his life was really all about. And the words to ignite the fires to light innocent minds and to boil the frog croaking those words inside him. Those would be real mental fireworks to heat the minds of his readers.

As a rule, he was careful speaking about such matters— mad deviations, mad inventions, mad conclusions—even with

Ute he was wary. Because then she always said that was why he had to switch to fiction. But the idea was frightening. Not the writing part; the digging into himself was his fear. The fear of learning what he really believed. More scary than was Stalingrad when it was happening. No, it was not the putting it on paper that scared him. He feared he would dig and dig and dig and then find he had gotten used to the idea of a Stalingrad being possible. Normal in the life of a man. That would be disaster.


## ERICA-ERIKA

On the kind of dark windy afternoon in Munich when you know the early morning rain is returning, Hannah dropped in to introduce her new friend, Erica.

"Erica!" Helmut exclaimed spontaneously as any German ex-wartime soldier might. "Her name is Erika?" He thought of her name with a "k" instead of a "c".

They both looked at him funny. As did Ute. He just shrugged, a strange look on his face. He would explain another day about the song.

Erica Valente was from Trento, the twenty-five year old daughter of Austrian parents, bi-lingual like Hannah. They were a striking couple of young women. Dark haired Hannah; blond Erica. Both taller than average Italian women. Though there was something Germanic about them, they both had a flamboyant Italian flair in dress and manners: their skirts a bit shorter, that extra something in dress such as Erica's red pumps and Hannah's multi-colored silken scarves. Still, Hannah, like her mother, was a bit more conservative. Today they only exchanged greetings with Helmut and Ute before they disappeared upstairs to Hannah's studio.

Back at his desk, Helmut stared out the windows for a long moment, a perplexed frown in his eyes. There was something disturbing about Erica, though he couldn't put his finger on what it was. He sensed discrepancies between her actions and her words. Flamboyantly show-off in one moment, shy in the next, And there was a certain reticence in her words, something unspoken about her. Something like his impressions of his friend, Ramon, the Romanian in Montagna in the Italian Alps: Ramon was ex-intelligence, worked also for Gehlen and for unexplained reasons regularly disappeared from Montagna. Erica's almost imperceptible manner of seeming to withhold her real self could seem to be timidity. Though they had just met, he didn't attribute her restraint to bashfulness; she was anything but demure. Such first impressions count, the former intelligence agent reminded himself. Still, in those few minutes together she had made the impression of one who lived life as if on the theater stage. She did smile too much … though often at the wrong time. And as it turned out she too, like Ramon, disappeared for days at a time.

"Hannichka, you don't help me to d*ipanare la matassa*, to untie the knot, that is Erica," he later complained to his daughter, using an Italian expression just to show off his acquired Italian that she knew like the native she nearly was.

"Papa, she's just a happy person. Doesn't know what a bad mood is." Hannah saw only joy in her girlfriend, whose mysterious absences she overlooked.

"Well, the way she just disappears from one day to the next is a knot that needs disentangling. I'm not blind, *Schatz* … I see you too are perplexed by her vanishing like that. And then she never explains."

"OK, Hannah, where is Erica this time?" Helmut asked his daughter another day when she sat staring at a painting propped on what seemed a lonely easel … in that moment as extraneous to the unfinished work as it was to her.

"Who knows? She left a note in my mailbox saying not to call her or even ask about her … that she would see me next Saturday, That is, today. Her usual signature, *see you later, alligator*."

"What's your friend up to, do you think?"

"I can't figure it out. She's always so open. Always. So this habit of just vanishing is simply *bizzarro.*"

"What do you say we take a walk, Hannah? Think things over. And I want to see Hohenzollern Strasse again."

"Again? Erica lives there, you know. Why? Have you been there before?"

"I lived on the street when I was a student …. before the war. So did a lot of artistic people in those times. Kandinski lived here. Had his studio down near Leopoldstrasse."

"I didn't know that. How wonderful to know."

"And for that matter so did Werner von Braun, the physicist, once a Nazi, I think, and one of the inventors of the atomic bomb … but on the side of the Americans. Didn't seem to care for whom he worked … on all those nasty projects. Used for mass murder against the Japanese. No morality at all in that man."

"But the bomb put an end to the war, no?"

"No! Hannah. No! The war with Japan was already won," he said, clearing his throat ever so carefully. "The Japanese were trying to surrender. Beaten and crushed like we were. The truth is that Braun's Ami bomb killed the Japanese as a message to the Russians … and as a test on real people. It was not to win the war more quickly. That's why they used it … Why, the Amis would have bombed their ally Russia instead of Japan if they'd had it a bit earlier."

"Cynic! Anyway, Papi, why this street now?"

"No matter. Just point out where she lives. On Hohenzollern Platz … I seem to remember. Hey, oh, my God, would you look at that. Even a metro station here on the *Platz*. I loved this street. But it's so different today The architecture resplendent, the cafés … and now the traffic that wasn't here before. And the metro station right here. The best city transportation in the world!"

"No, Papa, she doesn't live on the square. She has a small flat in a famous apartment building farther down … at number 58."

"You've been there often, I suppose?" he added looking off down Hohenzollern Strasse as if distracted. Which he was not.

"Yes, many times."

"Hannah, please listen to me. You have to stay away from there. Let her come to your place … but I hope you will avoid Hohenzollern Strasse 58."

"Papa! Why? Why would you say a thing like that? What is it? Are you jealous?"

"Hannah, my dear daughter. Please! Just stay away from her house. It's a hunch. Things are not what they seem. I know how some things work in this country."

"Well, you seem to know something I don't. Much more. So tell me. Then, well, we can talk about it."

"The thing is, Hannichka, we don't always tell everything about ourselves, do we? Maybe there's more to the story. Doesn't she have a man friend … at her age and so beautiful … with the world at her feet?"

"Oh, Papi, don't be so … so *albern*. So silly. I don't either … have a man friend, I mean. Not right now. Not since … well, not since Milano."

They stopped in front of number 58. Hannah pointed out a third floor window. "Erica's tiny apartment! Great location, no? I just love this street."

"How many apartments are on her floor anyway?" Helmut asked, studying the width and depth of the building and humming to himself *EEErikà*. "Maybe … just maybe she has more space than it seems."

"What do you mean? She has two rooms, the one that faces the street, then her bedroom and bath and the kitchen."

"Maybe there's an adjoining apartment. Something bigger. Have you ever seen her neighbors?"

"No, but I don't get what you're driving at? I know you have reservations about her ... but why your interest for the other apartments around her? Or is that your old intelligence syndrome showing?"

"Well, Hannah, I do have my past to deal with. But then there's also my work today. Erica told me she knew Renato Curcio in Trento ... also his wife, Mara Cagol. She also knew Alberto Franceschini. The Red Brigade founders! Then here in Munich appears this beautiful girl named Erica Valente from Trento. Lives most of the time in Munich. Is not even Italian, but Austrian. Has no official job. Happens to be bi-lingual like you, German and Italian. Keeps disappearing. I would bet she knows Andreas Baader too ... and Ulrike Meinhof and Gudrun Ensslin. Ask her about that... And they're all—the real RAF warriors—but all in prison.

"So now a second-generation Red Army militants—and Red Brigadists too— have taken over. And I fear they're supported by Gehlen-Gladio-NATO-American infiltrators who have different tasks altogether. They're the real danger for you. A police contact told me that even they have orders to go easy on them ... on the second generation. And Hannah, these militants seem more terrorists than revolutionaries. They're more violent too ... and less ideologically driven. They don't care a whit about moral restrictions. Nothing counts but them. And, Hannah—also their controllers. Controllers do exist. And controllers have their controllers ... many from across the Atlantic. Believe me. So that's why I ask you to stay away from here. You never know!"

"So what? You like the Baader-Meinhof people ... at least in your articles you never criticize them. You don't call them terrorists, as others do. You criticize our government, say they're all Nazis. So Papa, where do you really stand?"

"Well, aren't they? I *am* for RAF. For the real Red Army Faction. But I am NOT for those who become shock troops for the fascist government ... and for America's interests. Nazis or would-be Nazis actually run things again in our country anyway … and it's spreading. This is all so rotten, Hannichka. Just so rotten … at the very core. Evil. Bad for Germany. And to think I went to Stalingrad for this! And thousands of kids were there too. Kids went to die in Russia on orders from these people. Adult Germans were guilty, yes. Many! Most! They didn't just permit Hitler and the Nazis. They became supporters. They shared Nazi victories. Read Walter Benjamin and Bertold Brecht. Read our writers of today. Read Böll. Read Günther Grass. Read Ulrike Meinhof! Nazi hosannas filled the squares of Germany, then the squares and the piazzas of Europe. Sang their songs. The good soldiers sang *Erika*, about a little flower, a *Blümlein* in the heather, *EEErikà, und das heist... EEErika*, even if thinking of a girl back home. And people sang the Nazi anthem, the *Horst Wessel Lied, Die Fahne Hoch, die Reihen fest geschlossen*, nearly all arms raised in the Nazi salute. Believers. Kam'raden, die Rotfront und Reaktion erschossen, /Marschier'n im Geist/ In unser'n Reihen mit.

"They were the system … along with a lot of other Europeans and Americans. Americans perhaps more than others. But we Germans did much more than just go along with it. We were on the front. German people were the Nazi system …"

"But not just in Germany. We're not the only guilty."

"We? *You* are not guilty at all. Erica is not guilty. Your generation is not guilty. Mine is the guilty generation. And not only Germans. Nazis all over Europe and America helped. Where do you think all that money and support came from? Anything to smash Communism in Russia. Twenty-six million Russians dead, the Jews, the gypsies, the homosexuals and the political dissidents.

"But also many seventeen and eighteen year olds and younger, Germans and Russians, Italians and Romanians, paid for Nazism with their lives in the East. I had a friend in Stalingrad, who'd been a history professor before the war, in Cologne. He was sick on the subject … especially after we all knew the war was lost: *Just wait!* he said. *They'll be back. Give them a foothold, just leg room, and they'll return, like Erika flowers in the spring,* He knew his stuff. The most prescient person I've ever known. So today, just as he predicted, the Nazis and their heirs are back! Everywhere. Actually they never left. After all that, they're back in power.

"Nazis are again in German politics today. In government. In business. And many are slipping into the academic world. Many in journalism. They're sneaky, join secret societies, take bribes carefully. But they're there. Where I worked before we escaped to Italy, in the Gehlen Intelligence Org, they were *all* ex-Nazis. Still Nazis. But the Americans there, with their good humor in their bright smiling faces, they were the worst Nazis! Those with all their blessings, with their exceptionalism and their exoneration from the rules of others. And they're still that way. The SS is back. They didn't talk about it but they were that way. When I interviewed war prisoners returning from Russia, Germans like me, they were afraid I was the SS. In Montagna where you grew up, our Romanian friend became a double, a double agent, sent back to Communist Romania … by Nazis. A big wheel there today … and he works for us too. Trust is the word in today's world, Hannah. Trust. But nobody has it. Trust, I mean. Trusts means mistrust. Deception. Trust is an extant word. An unspoken word! Nobody trusts anybody. You know what the greatest modern discovery is? The traitor! Politically correct traitor. That is to say that a traitor is not necessarily your enemy. Not at all. In fact, he's your potential friend. Why? Because in our age, and where I once worked, you want to send him back to where he came from … as a double! So trust now means untrust. Crazy world, Hannah, dearest. Crazy! Your mother likes to say that the 'whole fucking world' is right-wing. Actually she uses the word 'Nazi' instead of right-wing. People like Ulrike Meinhof and Gudrun Ensslin understand. They are right. And yes, I feel, uh, well, I feel sympathy for them. No, I feel much more than mere sympathy. I feel love for them. But still, I don't want to  see you in jail with them now ... though like many people, I admire those who take that extra step ... like Ulrike and Gudrun ... and rebel against the whole system. The whole politically corrupt, Nazi-inclined, Ami-subservient system."

"Papa! Papa! You paint a black picture! A black picture of people ... and of my country. A country I'm just now trying to discover."

"That's both good and bad. Good you are learning the truth. But you must be careful. Very careful. Ok, Schatz, I agree. And there *are* things in life worth suffering for. Going to jail for. In some cases. But not needlessly. You can't help your country from a padded, sound-proof isolationist cell like Stammheim ... unless you're a  martyr. Unless you're like Zoya the Russian partisan in Russia: 'You can't hang us all.'  In a cell like where they're holding Ulrike Meinhof. Oh, yes, she's a hero ... for today. For a few people. For more than a few. But tomorrow even they too will have forgotten her. And her sacrifice will have been in vain."

"Wait! I have an idea. What do you say—if you can stay away from your canvases long enough. Let's get your mother and have lunch today at the Osteria Italiana over on Schelling Strasse. In memory of former times. *Va bene*?

"OK, but Erica is returning this morning. Supposed to come around noon ... if she gets back from wherever she was."

"Good, she's invited, too,"

## OSTERIA ITALIANA-HITLER'S FAVORITE MUNICH RESTAURANT

"Now beautiful ladies, here we are in this fine restaurant that they say Hitler loved. Opened in the early thirties, I think. Still a Nazi place? I don't really know. But the food is good. I think for years it was the only Italian restaurant in old München-Stadt. Speaking of Nazi places—words seldom spoken these days—we have to understand the situation in this country after the war … in order to understand ourselves. To understand other Europeans, and other peoples of the world too. That's the key. The Nazi was the key evil. The ur-Nazi, I mean to say. We know who they were! And I don't mean the Aryans as Hitler and that mad crowd believed. … and, you know, I really do love RAF!" he said, looking at Hannah, but, thinking of Erica. And of that song, *und das heisst ERIKA*!

He felt his loquacity on his lips. The power of pre-lunch vodka, he admitted to himself. The strength of one hundred camels in the courtyard, he thought, quoting some unknown Arab writer. The women stared at him, both curious and amused. Ute, too, but she nervously, urging him to lower his voice.

Helmut peered around the room of big windows, green curtains and red carpets spread here and there over polished parquet floors. He knew the other diners considered him some newly discovered caveman. Or a madman. The Munich effect, he called it.

The restaurant was quiet. Whispers from all corners. A tinkle of glass against glass. Heads bent over plates of pasta. Everyone pretending they didn't overhear him. Here and there a nearly finished tiramisu, an espresso, or simply hypnotically blank whiter than white tablecloths. He hoped his words hurt. He hoped he wouldn't be welcome another time. No one wanted to hear the words being spoken across the room for all. Words that should remain unspoken.

"The remaining young people of the post-war are really pissed at the older generation," Helmut added. "Official *denazification* was a farce. Former Nazis hold positions in government and the economy. The Communist Party was outlawed in 1956. Ex-Nazis everywhere, right down to the local level. They love the judiciary. Everybody knows. Adenauer, the first Federal Republic chancellor right up until 1963, appointed a former Nazi as Director of the Federal Chancellery. Conservatives run the media—the important mass-circulation tabloids are controlled by the same conservatives that permitted permanent Allied-U.S. occupation of the country and organizations like that of Reinhard Gehlen where I worked. I used to go to certain offices in the I.G. Farben building in Frankfurt miraculously untouched by Ami bombs. Gudrun Ensslin and Andreas Baader should have bombed it instead of the department store! Europe's biggest chemical multinational, used slave labor from Auschwitz while producing Zylon B to kill them in the gas chambers. Now it's office space for the victors. Oh, I.G. Farben was never their enemy … but an ally. And I know what they were doing after the war. Still full of Nazis. This time Ami Nazis. Then and then and then, then came the Grand Coalition between our two main parties, the Christian Democrats and the Socialists of the SPD controlling 95% of the Bundestag. And the former Nazi Party member, Kurt Georg Kiesinger, was chancellor. The real left was horrified. All that meant alliance with NATO and the USA. And then in 1972 the neo-Nazis passed a law, the *Radicalenerlass that banned radicals or those of* "questionable" political persuasion from jobs in the public sector. And still, there was the reality of the association of large parts of the post-war allegedly *denazified* society with Nazism. No wonder …"

"Still, Papa, Why RAF? Why all this violence? Why are Germans killing other Germans?"

"Why the violence? People remember that in the 1960s—while we were in Italy—German students engaged in endless debates about the use of violence. There were great demonstrations right here in Munich too. I took the night train up from Milano for one of them. Oh, yes, we need a movement, they said. Oh, but please, no violence. Peace marches should be more serious. But what did that mean? Longer columns marching over greater distances? More placards? Louder voices? General strikes? But still, just no violence. Why no violence? They thought violence meant war.

"Andreas Baader and Ulrike Meinhhof and Gudrun Ensslin stopped dancing and drinking champagne and took to smashing that comforting air of non-violence. The RAF of Andreas Baader and Ulrike Meinhof made those comfortable peace marches seem like afternoon tea parties. They exploded that nice tea party atmosphere in Germany … in Europe. Paris 1968 happened. And they threw cobblestones and called police pigs. But then RAF raised the bar higher. They showed the necessity of violence as the first step toward the revolution many wanted. RAF was the vanguard … the one Lenin meant. Quite legitimate, some Germans came to think.

"Why the violence, you ask?"

Helmut's voice had gradually risen. Ute shushed him.

Useless. Helmut Seifert was on a roll.

"RAF people rightfully call my generation pigs. The Auschwitz generation that wanted to kill all of them too. And so, Andreas and Gudrun and Ulrike armed themselves and then killed too. Officially RAF killed some thirty-four people from the time of its founding in 1970 … and twenty-seven of their own fell."

"Papa, Lower your voice. They're all listening."

"And that my dear is a problem. All the people here listen and whisper… But they're horrified and ashamed too. They know it's true. They're disturbed, Not by *my* voice. The good German people never raise their voices. The good people don't— like these here … the good law-abiding people keep their voices down. So, you don't know their real thoughts, they too are unspoken.

"But here's another thing: just imagine if they had raised their voices after the war. What might have happened here in, say the 1950s and 60s, if there'd been no U.S. military-CIA occupation? It's hard to know for certain but we Germans have to try to understand. The right people have to speak louder. For what has happened here is now happening all over Europe … And that, my dears, is what our Europe is all about. A Europe 'run' by the USA … without even the fiction of NATO or European Union, both staggering around in confusion … already on the verge of collapse. But a Europe without Ami occupation? How would it be? We should try to picture it."

"So how would it be?" Ute, Hannah and Erica talk all at once. People around the room looking their way … ever so discreetly … whispering one to the other, overhearing but not really understanding the words.

"Different. I like to think so anyway. I think of a Germany in some kind of a union of European peoples."

"But we have a union!" Ute says.

"We have a union of bureaucratic governments and institutions creating ever new bureaucracies staffed by super-paid Nazi-inclined bureaucrats. We need something different from what we have … on this, this gradually disappearing tip— just a tip, mind you—of the huge Eurasian continent. Hannicka, your mother once noted that we're not even a continent. Not at all. We're just a tip of land in the world of the planet Earth."

"A real union of European nations is what thinking people want for Europe," Ute said. "Germans, Italians and French."

"That's not what reformers do," Hannah added with a sigh.

"But it's what revolutionaries demand," Erica murmured, looking at the table and fiddling with a dessert spoon. "I suppose the first step has to be what you said, Herr Hartmann …"

"Helmut! Erica, my name is Helmut. That's another thing we have to get rid of … our exaggerated German formality. Are you too, of all people, going to call Ute, Frau Journalist Hartmann?"

"Sorry! But I meant it as a sign of respect. Anyway, Helmut, I agree." Then lowering her voice even more: "First, shut down NATO and send Ami troops home, then denazify all of Europe! And pay up for our past imperialism! Then we'll see who Europeans really are … if they will finally pay in full for the past centuries of Euro-imperialism. There! Well, now I've said it."

The others stared at Erica in silence, she lifted her eyes. Helmut locked his eyes into hers for long seconds before he said: "Thanks for that Erica. I understand … uh,  I understand you. We're in complete agreement. And moreover, we have to keep in mind that thus far this RAF is a very European kind of thing … chiefly a Central European matter. Do others know about our secret war here in Germany, in Italy,  too? I doubt it. Or not much … or don't understand it."

Another moment passed before he chuckled and added: "Ironic that this conversation is taking place in Hitler's favorite restaurant. The Italian restaurant in Munich, in Germany. And we just wanted a good Italian meal. Turned out better than we could have hoped for."

He looked around the table nervously. Around the room … as if for something to hold onto. "Uh, anyone for another espresso? Or should we order another round
of  Stalingradskaya vodka?"

## ULRIKE MARIE MEINHOF

«*Wirft man einen Stein, so ist das eine strafbare Handlung. Werden tausend Steine geworfen, ist das eine politische Aktion. Zündet man ein Auto an, ist das eine strafbare Handlung, werden hundert Autos angezündet, ist das eine politische Aktion. Protest ist, wenn ich sage, das und das paßt mir nicht.*

*Widerstand ist, wenn ich dafür sorge, daß das, was mir nicht paßt, nicht länger geschieht»* Ulrike Meinhof.

(You throw a stone, that is a crime. If a thousand stones are thrown, that is a political action. You set one car on fire, that is a crime. You set one hundred on fire, that's a political action. Protest is when I say I do not like this or that. Resistance is when I act so that that which I do not like, no longer occurs.)

For Helmut Seifert the young journalist turned revolutionary was a hero: Ulrike Meinhof, born October 7, 1934 in Oldenburg (Germany), died May 9, 1976 in Stammheim Prison in Stuttgart). Journalist, revolutionary and co-founder of the Red Army Faction. She would be celebrated in song, literature and film because she lived intensely and died like a corralled steer, a prisoner of the state against which she fought. Officially, a "suicide; for Helmut she was assassinated by the state ... strangled and hanged during the night on the bars of her cell window.

She wrote in an essay in number 14, 1968 of *Konkret* about the Frankfurt department store fire set by Gudrun Ensslin: *The progressive moment in a department store fire is not in the destruction of the goods; it lies in the criminality of the action ... in the breaking of the law.* (**Das progressive Moment einer Warenhausbrandstiftung liegt nicht in der Vernichtung der Waren, es liegt in der Kriminalität der Tat, im Gesetzesbruch.**)

And in the national weekly, *Der Spiegel*, number 25, of 15 June 1970: *"Naturally we call cops pigs. We say the one in uniform is a pig, not a person, and so we have to fight him. That means we cannot speak with him for it is wrong even to speak with such people, and naturally shots may be fired."* (Wir sagen, natürlich, die Bullen sind Schweine, wir sagen, der Typ in der Uniform ist ein Schwein, das ist kein Mensch, und so haben wir uns mit ihm auseinanderzusetzen. Das heißt, wir haben nicht mit ihm zu reden, und es ist falsch überhaupt mit diesen Leuten zu reden, und natürlich kann geschossen werden.")


## AGAIN IN THE OSTERIA ITALIANA


Helmut and Ute together with Hannah and Erica were sitting this time in a secluded corner table of what they all now ironically referred to as "Hitler's favorite restaurant." Only a few days had passed since the suicide-murder of Ulrike Meinhof. Erica looked shaken, bewildered and fearful. Helmut thought RAF, he thought Erica. Never Baader-Meinhof Gang. RAF it was. And Erica was somehow involved.

After a long silence while he gazed at only sullen faces around them, all seeming to be looking at him and waiting, he suddenly shouted: "Ulrike Meinhof was in the direct anti-systemic ideological line of Rosa Luxemburg and Sophie Scholl. Ulrike paid with her life for her anti-imperialism and anti-Nazism—as did Sophie and Rosa—not for her crimes. They are heroes. RAF, I mean. Or nearly all of them. One problem is there are always traitors. And traitors are dangerous," he said, looking  hard at Erica. And in his mind seeing Hannah's friend's name written with a "c". Not the Germanic "k". Though it would change nothing, nor would it bring Ulrike back to life, still he often imagined Erica, too, as heroic.

"Ulrike led a normal life before her fateful choice for violence. She loved dancing at balls in the Hotel Vierjahreszeiten in Hamburg and drinking expensive champagne. She was sentimental in a bourgeois way" Helmut said, (just as later the artist Gerhard Richter would define her in his comments about his fifteen-painting cycle of RAF leaders, *October 18, 1977.*)

"But Ulrike's mind worked in a different manner," Helmut goes on unrelentingly. "She thought we Germans had to change. She couldn't accept a neo-Nazi Germany. As a student she turned every subject upside down. She was disturbing. Eventually she became an editor at the Communist magazine, *Konkret*, married its publisher, Klaus Rainer Röhl, had two children. Pages on folio heavy stock of the biweekly were plastered on the walls of student rooms … like those of Che Guevara today. Editor-in-chief of *Konkret* was not enough. She wanted action. Violence was necessary. But Klaus didn't share her beliefs. They divorced and the magazine dissolved over the use of violence. [7]

"And Ulrike? Disgusted with the inertia of the left, she joined what became the RAF, went to Jordan for arms training with the PLO and returned ready for action. Armed attacks on capitalist symbols and U.S. military bases—likely the latter marking her ultimate downfall. After two years of preliminary hearings she was sentenced to eight's year imprisonment. Eventually however she, Andreas Baader, Gudrun Ensslin and Jan-Karl Raspe were jointly charged with four counts of murder, fifty-four attempted murders and criminal association, But before the trial's conclusion Ulrike was found hanged in her cell on May 6, 1976. She would have gotten a life sentence as the others did. Though she officially hanged herself with rope fashioned from a towel, many Germans have never believed it. Her burial in Berlin-Mariendorf six days after her death turned into a demonstration of four thousand people.

"Ulrike Meinhof died young but she left behind a long legacy of writing and films by leading filmmakers like Margaretha von Trotta[8].… but also, sadness and desperation in our German state."

**GUDRUN ENSSLIN**
**HELMUT'S NOTES: ANDREAS BAADER**
**AND THE ROTE ARME FAKTION**

First of all, Seifert—as Helmut liked to call himself—kept in mind that RAF was a group of revolutionaries. Not terrorists. Not a gang of criminals. Second, RAF was run by extraordinary and courageous women—women like also Sophie Scholl during Nazism in Munich, women committed to social-political change—unlike the Red Brigades in Italy run chiefly by men, but who, like RAF, were also revolutionaries. Third, RAF like the Red Brigades was violent. Gudrun Ensslin wrote: *"Violence is the only answer to violence."* And: *"This is the Auschwitz generation, and there's no arguing with them! "*

Gudrun Ensslin became one of the most "wanted" persons in Germany. She was born in 1940 in the village of Bartholomä in Baden-Württemberg, the daughter of a Protestant Pastor. At age eighteen she studied a year in the USA in Warren, Pennsylvania, then did American and German studies in the University of Tübingen. After a first marriage and the birth of a son, she met Andreas Baader, widely known as "a criminal from Munich". Andreas became the man of her life. Student protest against the  visit of the Shah of Iran was then a turning point: the acquittal of the policeman who shot and killed a young student, Benno Ohnesorg, outraged her. Consequently she moved farther and farther left and finally opened battle on the "fascist" West German state. She and Andreas firebombed a Frankfurt am Main department store, for which they were arrested in 1968 and sentenced to prison. Gudrun appealed the sentence and was released in 1969. She bolted and went underground and helped Andreas escape. At that point the die was cast. In May of 1970: she wrote: *I like the great things you can buy in a department store. But when you have to buy them in order to stay unaware, comatose, then the price you pay is too high."*

As the existence of RAF became known for its robberies and violence, the media referred to it as the Baader-Meinhof Gang. In reality, like Josef Vissarionivich

Djugashvili (Stalin), they robbed banks to finance their new organization, the Red Army Faction. Andreas and Gudrun were in action until 1972 when they and other RAF members were again arrested.

The state's ferocious response to RAF—its disproportionate response—actually legitimized them. People who might have thought they were just a minor criminal group, an annoyance, became aware of them. People then learned a lot from the great Stammheim show trial of the RAF members. People learned their government considered the RAF such a huge threat to society that it was ready to limit civil liberties to stop them. Actually, (and here Helmut's notes were underlined): Actually, the Baader-Meinhof Group trial was a false flag operation. For the damage done by RAF was slight as compared to the day-to-day crimes of a whole society. The government reaction to the group's actions was massive. So how could average people be dismissive of them if their government spent so much energy into stopping them ... then killing them? The Baader-Meinhof trial of Andreas Baader, Ulrike Meinhof, Gudrun Ensslin and Jan-Karl Raspe—after they had been in isolation for three years—lasted over a year, up to the time of Ulrike Meinhof's death in prison. From May 1975 it went on: hordes of lawyers and judges many of whom ex-Nazis; official leaks to the press of illegally taped conversations between defendants and lawyers; a specially built courtroom on the grounds of Stammheim Prison. For the people this was more than a show trial. It was a theatrical presentation intended to sway a whole nation.

Andreas Baader and companions were all prisoners in Stammheim. In isolation. Soundproof cells. The second RAF generation had taken over the action outside. They were even more violent. Doing what they could for the release of their jailed companions, in 1977 they abducted the President of West German Industrialists and an ex-SS officer, Hans-Martin Schleyer and offered an exchange. The government refused. So they hijacked a Lufthansa Boeing737 on October 17, and landed in Mogadishu and tried to negotiate with police from there. But no deal. No negotiations with terrorists! Finally, Special Forces erupted into the parked plane, saved the passengers and killed the "terrorists". As payback, RAF killed Schleyer. Then on the very next day, in the Stammheim prison Baader and Gudrun Ensslin were found dead in their cells and a third, Jan-Karl Raspe died in a hospital. The two men were shot, Gudrun, strangled with the cable from a loudspeaker and hanged from her cell's window bars.

The official version of suicide has never been popularly believed in Germany. People believe they were executed, as did I, Helmut Seifert Hartmann: "They were assassinated by the state."

The night of October 18, 1977 came to be called 'Death Night', the night three key members of the first generation of the Red Army Faction died in mysterious circumstances in the Stammheim Prison in Stuttgart. (Like the author, Helmut Seifert believes they were murdered by the state.) A fourth survived severe stab wounds. The high-jacked plane, the special forces assault in Mogadishu, the death of the revolutionaries, and the murder of Schleyer a former rabid SS officer, marked the climax of the German Autumn and the RAF attacks on the Nazi-infested state.

The author finds the most fascinating the figure of Gudrun Ensslin, Baader's companion and co-founder of the urban guerilla "army" … and one of those who died on Death Night. Gudrun's history was the history of her era. One of the two women who made RAF. For her the RAF embodied the essence of "the duty of resistance" to the U.S.-created German Federal Republic.

Helmut too now saw it for what it was: contrary to popular thought of Germany as a shining example of post-1945, he saw West German democracy as an ex-Nazi led society. The German society the USA had wanted in Germany since Nazism's assumption of power in 1933. The society of those Nazi protégés of the USA who were never *denazified*. Most likely *undenazifiable*. Whose Nazi past was ignored. They were RAF's blood enemies.

# Historical Notes

(1) Literary historian and critic Nicola Chiaromonte's major work is one long commentary on the role of fiction: the novels of Stendhal, Tolstoy, Roger Martin du Gard, Malraux, and Pasternak. "Only through fiction and the imaginary," he writes, "can we learn something real about individual experience. What we learn is that individual experience refutes historical optimism. Chiaromonte contends that the works of Stendhal et al. make up a tradition: the antihistorical novel, in which the idea of History as rational and progressive is shown to be an illusion. From his own experience in exile in the twenty years of Italian Fascism, Chiaromonte could write this: "In the beginning there was the lie." He believed that the sense of history begins in the lie, "an irresistible prevalence of the false over the authentic, of betrayal over loyalty, of cowardice over courage." His lifetime theme was the relationship between man and the event, between what one believes and what happens to him. Some of his essays included in his collection, *To Believe and Not To Believe (Credere e Non Credere)*, were presented at Princeton in 1966 when he held the Christian Gauss Seminars On Literary Criticism. No one has ever before linked these authors in quite this way; whatever the merits of Chiaromonte's argument as political philosophy, as literary criticism it is a brilliant conception.

In Stendhal's *The Charterhouse of Parma* the young Fabrizio del Dongo sets out to join Napoleon's army. What happens is his farcical search for the war: he is robbed and jailed as a spy, taken in by a woman who outfits him in a dead Hussar's uniform and sends him off to the battle at Waterloo. Fabrizio wanders around the battlefield, alternately delighted and horrified, never comprehending what is happening and if this is really war. And in fact the event as Stendhal describes it is incomprehensible— even, it seems, to Napoleon and his marshals, who gallop around with little purpose or effect.

Though Chiaromonte does not mention Camus in his essay *The Paradox of History*, he was influenced by *The Rebel;* in Rome he spoke to me of his admiration for Albert Camus. Chiaromonte concentrated on art and literature. He did not appreciate high-flown prose style and programmatic detail. Like Camus he stressed limits and consequently Mediterranean mèsure. Together they are  the dernier cri of 20th century literary radicalism: their  attempt to derive from art a criticism of politics and an explanation of the apparently inexplicable history of this century.

(2) Helmut Hartmann still sees Europe the way it had always been and as he thought it was supposed to be. He had lived a life in which the mad visions of a few became the delusions of many, the illusions of the masses and the tragedy of a people. Such was also the foreign image of Old Europe, which in reality was even more corrupt and colonialist-imperialist with an irrepressible predilection for war. Yet tourists loved it that way, just as did some of Europe's own intellectuals as well as artists of the world who felt Europe was the only place to be. That variegated multiethnic semi-continent of Europe was a world. The so-called Iron Curtain that came down to mark the start of the Cold War after WWII only reinforced the continental image of this incomprehensible Europe, with an enticing ideological taint of danger attached.

(3) At the end of WWII in 1945 the East European expert Major General Reinhard Gehlen became part of the CIA which promptly organized and financed the Gehlen Group, or Gehlen Org, for intelligence and espionage activities against the USSR. The spymaster Reinhard Gehlen had ties to extreme rightist organizations like Stepan Bandera's fascist Organization of Ukrainian Nationalists; Romania's Iron Guard and the Ustashe of Yugoslavia. After Hitler fired Gehlen during the war in Russia because of his negative reports, Gehlen buried in watertight cans his files on the Red Army. On

May 22, 1945, Gehlen and top aides surrendered to the American Counter-intelligence Corps. Since the USA needed Soviet military experts, Gehlen was removed from prisoner-of-war rolls and placed in charge of a group of Germans gathering intelligence for the USA. Unrepentant Nazis occupied key posts in his CIA affiliated, anticommunist "Gehlen Organization" headquartered in Munich-Pullach. Many people in Munich knew about the Gehlen Org but no one cared a whit. Later, the CIA named Reinhard Gehlen the first chief of the Intelligence Service of the U.S.-occupied German Federal Republic of West Germany, the *Bundesnachrichtendienst*, BND, 1956-68. During the Cold War period he was always a loyal executor of U.S. policies. General Gehlen was a very smart cookie. He died in 1979 in Starnberg near Munich.

(4) Nazi Germany annexed Sudetenland, part of Czechoslovakia, in September 1938 with the agreement of the Czechs who wanted to get rid of the two to three million ethnic Germans living there and with the agreement of the Allied powers of Great Britain and France. Hitler's troops had already marched into Austria in March 1938. Both annexations were part of Hitler's policies of uniting European Germans and expanding the territory (Lebensraum) of his Third Reich. These millions of Sudeten Germans—many of whom well-disposed toward Nazi Germany—were resettled in Germany proper. In this story, Helmut Hartmann is one such.

(5) Nicolae Ceausescu (1899-1989), a Romanian Communist politician, member of Politburo from 1954, President of the Romanian Socialist Republic from 1967-1989. During the Romanian anticommunist Revolution in 1989 that exploded in the big city of Timisoara with its strong Hungarian minority, on December 22 of that year he and his wife Elena Ceausescu were arrested in the small city of Targoviste near Bucharest, tried for genocide in a show trial, and executed on Christmas Day of 1989. The author remembers well a planned midnight bus trip

to Romania organized by Hungarians for foreign journalists in the country at the time, departure from Budapest on December 22. The trip was cancelled at the last minute because of the intensity of the fighting when everyone moving was a target by one or the other of the many diverse factions. I, like other journalists present in Budapest, was relieved we did not go, though I have always wondered who gave the order not to send us there. Now I wonder if my conceptual Ramon found refuge in America as did a long line of Nazis after WWII. Possible but not probable. Maybe he is back in Montagna that he so loved.

(6) The renowned German painter, Gerhard Richter painted a cycle of fifteen works of the Baader-Meinhof leaders in the infamous Stammheim Prison in Stuttgart shortly before their deaths, and some after they died, all murdered by the state, as popularly believed, or, officially, by their own hand. Known as *18 October, 1977* the works were shown in a widely publicized exhibition in the New York Museum of Modern Art (MOMA). Three young German radicals, members of the militant Baader-Meinhof Group, were found dead in a Stuttgart prison; they were pronounced suicides, but many people suspected they had been murdered. Gerhard Richter, one of the most exceptional and highly regarded artists of the second half of the 20th century, created these paintings eleven years after this traumatic event. They are among the most challenging works of the artist's career, and one of the 20th century's most famous works on a political theme, still highly debated and unsettling to this day. The paintings are based on newspaper and police photographs of moments in the lives and deaths of the four leaders of the Red Army Faction (RAF), the German left-wing revolutionary group that perpetrated a number of kidnappings and killings throughout the 1970s. The bodies of the three principal RAF members were found in the cells of the German prison of Stammheim where they were incarcerated. Richter's reworking of these documentary sources is dark, blurred, and diffuse. The cycle begins with a canvas based on a studio portrait photograph of Ulrike Meinhof, journalist turned radical

ideologue, an image that shows her as young and vital, but also, as the artist described, "sentimental in a bourgeois way." Paintings 2 through 7 shift tone abruptly, offering up the dead in paintings based on forensic photographs. There are three images of Meinhof, her body seen close-up, after she was found in her prison cell, the wound on her neck left by the noose visible, though softened by Richter's blur—as if he wanted to provide a buffer protecting us from the trauma of seeing it or offer her a modicum of privacy in death. Two paintings show Andreas Baader, splayed on the floor of his prison cell as he had fallen after shooting himself with a gun smuggled into the prison. Paintings 8 and 9 depict the interior of Baader's empty cell, the first showing his overflowing bookcase, and the other the record player that was reportedly used to smuggle in the gun with which Baader shot himself, so that these tokens of a classical cultural inheritance and knowledge take on a malevolent aspect. And one picture depicts Gudrun Ensslin, whose body, hanging from the bars of her prison window, was discovered on the morning of October 19. Our shock at seeing these corpses, bodies rendered lifeless from self-destructive violence, Richter suggests, may reflect the way we have weaned ourselves away from recognizing death with "our nice, tidy lifestyle." appreciation of [our time], to see it as it is." Paintings 10 and 11 show the arrest of Baader and Meins as it was broadcast on television to an audience of millions, with Meins forced to undress in front of the rolling cameras to show he was unarmed, the trace of his figure a tiny vertical blur in Richter's canvases. Paintings 12, 13, and 14 offer a trio of police images of Gudrun Ensslin in prison uniform in a photographic lineup, one in which she has enigmatic smile on her lips. And, finally, 15, the largest, depicts the funeral and burial of Baader, Ensslin, and Jan-Carl Raspe, another leader of the group. While Richter had previously chosen images related to Germany's recent history— he was among the first to introduce subjects from its Nazi past into artworks—he hadn't done so in many years. The October cycle was, as he put it, "a reversion" in both topic and technique. In remembering this particular episode, he touched on a topic that was still raw, still taboo in public dialogue despite the omnipresent media images that served as source material for the paintings: the dead terrorists remained largely unacknowledged, unmentioned, unmourned. "I was impressed by the terrorists' energy, their uncompromising determination and their absolute bravery," Richter reflected on this cataclysmic climax of opposing forces. "But I could not find it in my heart to condemn the state for its harsh response. That is what States are like, and I have known other, more ruthless ones." Richter may have felt this ambivalence particularly keenly. He was born in Dresden in 1932, the year before the Nazi rise to power, and witnessed the devastating bombing of that city as a young teenager. His first experience as an artist was in the newly founded German Democratic Republic, where he was trained in the propagandistic realism , but—with several trips to the West, including one to take in the great post-war showcase of international art at Documenta in Kassel—he crossed over permanently in 1961, the year the Berlin Wall was erected. His dual formation, split as it was between East and West Germany, left Richter highly attuned to the tensions, ironies, and fractures between two ideological systems, and harboring a deep skepticism about doctrines of any kind. "It was", he wrote in 1988, "a profound distaste for all claims to possess the truth." Richter acknowledged how profoundly unsettling he found the events around the Baader-Meinhof Group: "The deaths of the terrorists, and the related events both before and after," he reflected, "stand for a horror that distressed me and has haunted  me as unfinished business ever since, despite all my effort to repress it." Perhaps as a way of processing things, Richter began to collect materials related to the group, holding onto "a number of them" for years before he began painting the October cycle, filed under the heading of "unfinished business". In fact over 100 images related to the Baader-Meinhof Group appear in *Atlas*, Richter's ongoing scrapbook-like compendium of photographic source material.

When he began working in earnest on what would become *18 October 1977*, Richter drew some of his source images from newspapers and magazines or snapshots of television coverage—markers of the pervasiveness of media coverage of the Baader-Meinhof Group during their violent reign and in its aftermath. But others, taken from police photographs, were far less readily available, and serve as tokens of Richter's preoccupation with the topic and his determined research efforts in preparation for painting. The pictures of Ensslin offers no background information that would convey a politically charged meaning for the picture. The woman appears at first isolated and alone. However, the *confrontation 1, confrontation 2, confrontation 3* – contain a plethora of sides to be perceived. Richter slows down the progression of cinematic frames to an absolute standstill in the *confrontation* sequence. We see Gudrun Ensslin turning to engage with the viewer in the first piece, then looking at those who are taking her picture, and then turning away with a downcast head. Each picture portrays the same woman revealing different sides of her face while obscuring her meaning. If these frames showing an image were sequenced in milli-seconds as in a film, then perhaps her mouth would move, or her eyes would convey a sentiment … Richter destabilizes our view of Ensslin by making this very refusal to make meaning the focus of the work. He punches holes into any possible meaning that the woman could express by leaving the viewer with a refusal to reply which is initiated by Ensslin's refusal to speak in the first place. As a result, the appearance of the pictures is the focal point, or lack thereof, in Richter's art. He intends to paint the appearance of reality thereby capturing the multiple facets of the «passing-by» of experience. However, Richter anchors this moment of passing-by in attaching it to the empathetic experience of man in the *confrontation* series which appears attached to the viewer through the empathetic experience: «art serves to establish community. It links us with others, and with the things around us, in a shared vision and effort». Her moment of passing-by announces our perception of the art in which we confront what she has *already* seen. Thus, her experience finds its anchor in the viewer's gaze.

(7) After Ulrike Meinhof's arrest in 1972, Hermann L. Gremliza founded a new far-left *Konkret* magazine based in Hamburg for which he wrote the introductory column and to which a long line of German leftist intellectuals have contributed: such as Heinrich Böll, Daniel Cohn-Bandit, Rudi Dutschke, Hans Magnus Enzenberger, Jürgen Elsässer. Günter Grass, Sahra Wagenknecht.

(8) Films: In 1981 Margarethe von Trotta's feature film, *Marianne and Juliane*, is a portrait of the incarcerated Gudrun Ensslin. Five years later, Sabine Wegner played Ensslin in Reinhard Huff's *Stammheim,* a detailed account of the trial of Ensslin, Baader, Meinhof and others. In that same 1986, Corinna Kirchhoff played Ensslin in Markus Imhof's *The Journey*. In 1997, Anya Hoffmann was Ensslin in Heinrich Breloer's award winning TV drama, *Todespiel*. Gudrun Ensslin was played by Johanna Wokalek in Uli Edel's 2008 film, *The Baader Meinhof Complex*, the adaptation of a non-fiction book of the same name by Stefan Aust. Wokalek's performance was a nomination for the 2009 German Film Awards and a Bambi award as best German actress. The film was chosen as Germany's submission to the 81st Academy Awards for Best Foreign Language Film and was nominated for the 66th Golden Globe Awards. *Wer wenn nicht wir* (If not us, who), in which Lena Lauzemis plays Gudrun Ensslin, won the Alfred Bauer Prize and the Prize of the German Art House Cinemas at the Berlin International Film Festival of 2011.

*The End*